THE TRUE STORY
of
NED KELLY'S
LAST STAND

THE TRUE STORY

of

NED KELLY'S

LAST STAND

*New revelations unearthed about the
bloody siege at Glenrowan*

PAUL TERRY

ALLEN&UNWIN

SYDNEY · MELBOURNE · AUCKLAND · LONDON

First published in 2012

Allen & Unwin
Sydney, Melbourne, Auckland, London

83 Alexander Street
Crows Nest NSW 2065
Australia
Phone: (61 2) 8425 0100
Fax: (61 2) 9906 2218
Email: info@allenandunwin.com
Web: www.allenandunwin.com

Cataloguing-in-Publication details are available
from the National Library of Australia
www.trove.nla.gov.au

Published with assistance from the State Library of Victoria
slv.vic.gov.au

ISBN 978 1 74331 006 9
Set in 12.5/17.5 pt Bembo by Post Pre-press Group, Australia
Printed in Australia by Griffin Press

10 9 8 7 6 5 4 3 2 1

The paper in this book is FSC® certified.
FSC® promotes environmentally responsible,
socially beneficial and economically viable
management of the world's forests.

WATCH VIDEOS OF THE ARCHEOLOGICAL DIG WHILE YOU READ

QR Codes like the one above are placed throughout this book to bring videos taken during the archeological dig at the Glenrowan Inn site directly to your phone.

To watch these videos, simply download the free QR Code scanner at http://get.beetagg.com/en/qr-reader/download

Then hold your phone's camera a few inches away from the QR Code images and you'll immediately be taken into the action.

CONTENTS

FOREWORD

Ian Jones

When Paul Terry told me in 2007 that he planned to film a documentary on the upcoming archaeological excavation of the Glenrowan Inn site, I gladly offered my support.

I knew Paul as a talented television journalist and news producer at Prime TV. With his own cameraman and sound recordist he planned to cover the entire dig, which was to be conducted by Adam Ford—an archaeologist with an international reputation. Before work began, Paul and I discussed a historical wish-list—the ground plan of the inn, remnants of vanished Kelly Gang weapons, evidence from the room where the bodies of Gang members Dan Kelly and Steve Hart had been incinerated . . . anything that could illuminate the remarkable thirty-six hours between the gang's first moves to secure the town and their enemies' end play—burning the hotel.

Every time I visited the dig, Paul was there with his crew, meticulously documenting its progress. It was in the closing stages, shortly before the dig site was filled in again, that

Renegade Films appeared as production partners, with the suggestion that Tony Robinson of the internationally popular *Time Team* television series could be available to host the film. It is tempting to say that the rest is history. More accurately, the rest of the story, as it is known, was packaged as history. The site was re-opened, re-dug, the work was re-filmed, the story to be re-told as an attractive and successful television project, *Ned Kelly Uncovered*, expertly written and directed by Alex West of Renegade Films and presented with Tony Robinson's quirky and provocative style. Then, for the second time the excavated site of the inn was re-covered.

Now, this book marks Paul Terry's return to the project, sharing his observations of the original dig but also setting out in parallel to uncover the whole story of the gang's thirty-six hours in Glenrowan.

Paul had watched hundreds of artefacts emerge—delicately coaxed from the soil and charcoal, gently and painstakingly cleaned—to be studied and interpreted. He has now done the same with countless facets of the siege's story, helping to build a fresh and precisely detailed narrative into which the archaeology fits like pieces of a jigsaw.

This is much more than the story of how a major historical site—Australia's only surviving battlefield—was excavated; much more than the story of the battle that took place here and of the eight people who died as a result of it and the ninety who survived. This is the story of how a legend was born; a legend that still divides a nation.

Glenrowan is the most intricately documented phase of the Kelly story. It received saturation press coverage; three newspaper reporters and a press artist were on hand for the entire siege—from the first police charge, scattered by a volley from the armoured Kelly Gang, to the collapse of the Glenrowan Inn's blazing ruins.

Many of the police present and some of the gang's hostages gave evidence before a Royal Commission whose minutes, reports and appendices were packed into some 1000 closely printed pages. More reams of evidence emerged in the trial brought by police against the inn's publican, Ann Jones, for harbouring the gang, with still more evidence from the subsequent inquiry that won her compensation for the destruction of her hotel.

Most of the principal characters were extensively interviewed for years to come, some wrote articles, a few produced books. Even Ned Kelly was interviewed about his plans for Glenrowan and the events of the siege. He also produced a series of Condemned Cell letters to the Colony's governor, packed with obvious misinformation about the siege that is like an old-fashioned maternity smock—advertising what it sets out to hide.

Topped off with letters to various editors, affidavits, local and family traditions and an ever-growing library of books, the events of Glenrowan provide a minefield for academics and popular authors alike. Many follow a well-trodden path that weaves around the most threatening areas. Some create an anti-gravity pathway that enables them to skim over the ground with enormous confidence and a total lack of contact.

Paul Terry takes the most demanding course. He steps carefully into the minefield and treats each mine with the care it deserves. He identifies it, examines it, sometimes disposes of it or leaves it where it lies. We follow him with confidence.

Few have written about Ned Kelly with such balance and with so few preconceptions. Weighing this huge mass of material, Paul readily confronts the contradictions that emerge from both sides of the Kelly divide. A seemingly ruthless plan to wipe out a large force of pursuing police cannot be glossed over. Nor can an act of moral and physical courage that demanded almost superhuman endurance. Such is the nature of the Kelly story and its polarising power.

Here you will find no lofty and simplistic conclusions about Ned Kelly's central role in this Wagnerian final act. Paul ignores the need for the hero or villain of popular cliché. He portrays a man who shapes his own fate from his obsessions, from his inflexibility and, eventually, from an impulse that defies analysis and almost demands disbelief. Yet, in the end, scraps of charcoal, flattened lead, dented steel, damaged bone, bloodstained silk and—perhaps most vividly—one tiny shard of metal all insist we believe in the reality of what Ned Kelly attempted here. And try to understand what he achieved.

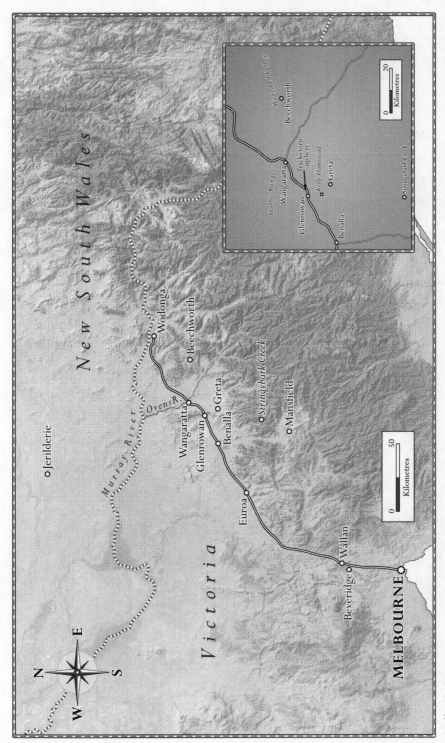

Kelly Country

TIMELINE: NED KELLY

1842

2 Jan   John 'Red' Kelly arrives in Van Diemen's Land from Ireland

1850

15 Nov   Marriage of John 'Red' Kelly and Ellen Quinn

1854

June   Ann Kennedy (Jones) arrives in Australia from Ireland
3 Dec   Miners' revolt at the Eureka Stockade
Dec/Jan   Birth of Ned Kelly

1866

             Ned rescues Richard Shelton at Avenel
28 Dec   Death of John 'Red' Kelly

1867

May   Ellen Kelly and family move to Greta

1869

Feb   Harry Power escapes from gaol and visits the Kelly family. Power recruits Ned as apprentice bushranger.

1870

5 June   Harry Power captured
10 Nov   Ned gaoled for three months over McCormick/ Gould incident

1871

Mar   Ned released from gaol
Apr   Ned arrested by Constable Hall. Kelly 'throws Hall in dust'.
May   Ned gaoled for three months for receiving stolen horse from 'Wild' Wright

1874

Feb	Ellen Kelly marries George King
Feb	Ned released from gaol
Aug	Ned and 'Wild' Wright fight at Beechworth

1878

	Ann Jones builds the Glenrowan Inn
15 Apr	Fitzpatrick Incident. Ned and Dan Kelly flee to the Wombat Ranges.
9 Oct	Ellen Kelly gaoled for three years for attempted murder of Fitzpatrick
26 Oct	Three police shot dead at Stringybark Creek
15 Nov	Kelly Gang outlawed
9–10 Dec	Kelly Gang raids Euroa; robs National Bank

1879

8–10 Feb	Kelly Gang raids Jerilderie. Jerilderie Letter released.

1880

26 June	Murder of Aaron Sherritt near Beechworth
26–28 June	Kelly Gang takes over Glenrowan. Siege and Last Stand at the Glenrowan Inn.
July	Ann Jones erects rough hut on siege site
6 Aug	Ned's committal hearing at Beechworth
28–29 Oct	Ned's trial in Melbourne
10 Nov	Ann Jones arrested for harbouring outlaws
11 Nov	Ned hanged in Melbourne

1881

Mar	Royal Commission hears first evidence

1882

17 Apr	Death of Jane Jones
	Ann Jones builds new hotel on siege site

1904

	Second hotel on siege site destroyed by fire

1910

          Wine shanty built on siege site

7 Oct   Death of Ann Jones

1976

          Wine shanty demolished. Site permanently
             unoccupied.

2008

          Excavation of inn site

2011

          Remains of Ned Kelly formally identified

TIMELINE: SIEGE

SATURDAY 26 JUNE

6.00–6.30 pm   Joe Byrne and Dan Kelly murder Aaron Sherritt near Beechworth

9.00 pm   Ned Kelly and Steve Hart arrive in Glenrowan; fail to pull up railway line

SUNDAY 27 JUNE

12.00–1.00 am   Roadworkers and Ann Jones taken hostage

1.00–2.00 am   Stanistreet family taken hostage

Railway workers Reardon and Sullivan taken hostage

3.00 am   Reardon begins to remove railway lines

6.00 am   Ned accepts Ann's invitation to breakfast

6.30 am   Police emerge from Sherritt's hut

9.00 am   Glenrowaners, including Tom Cameron and John Delaney, taken hostage

11.00 am   Curnow family taken hostage. Men held at the Glenrowan Inn, women and children at the Stanistreet's home.

Noon   Games begin in rear yard of the inn. Men hold a dance later that afternoon.

1.00 pm   Constable Armstrong arrives at Beechworth from Sherritt's hut to raise the alarm

2.30 pm   Superintendents Hare and Sadleir told of Sherritt murder

4.00 pm   Women and children brought to inn. Dance and party begin.

10.00 pm   Ned takes Hugh Bracken hostage. Curnow family released.

Police train leaves Melbourne

Party continues at the inn

SUNDAY 28 JUNE

2.00 am	Police train leaves Benalla
	Party ends. Ned decides to release hostages. Ann calls for Ned to give a lecture and hostages remain.
2.30 am	Curnow warns pilot engine driver near Glenrowan
3.00 am	Train pulls into Glenrowan station
	Hugh Bracken escapes
3.15–5.00 am	Shooting starts. Ned, Joe, and Francis Hare wounded.
	Johnny and Jane Jones, Martin Cherry and George Metcalf wounded.
	Signal rockets fired
	Constable Phillips overhears conversation between Ned and Joe
	Most of the hostages, including the Jones family and some of the Reardon family, escape.
	Ned leaves hotel to warn sympathisers. Battle continues.
6.00 am	Ned returns to hotel. Joe Byrne killed. Ned leaves hotel and meets Tom Lloyd.
6.15 am	Remaining Reardon family members attempt to flee. Sergeant Steele shoots Michael Reardon.
7.00 am	Ned fights Last Stand. Ned captured.
	Dan wounded in exchange of shots
10.00 am	Police call ceasefire. Most of the remaining hostages flee, except for wounded Martin Cherry.
12.00–12.30 pm	Father Gibney arrives at Glenrowan. Speaks to Ned.
	Maggie Skillian, Kate Kelly and 'Wild' Wright arrive at Glenrowan.
1.00 pm	Last shots fired from the inn

3.00 pm	Police set fire to the inn
	Gibney and police enter burning inn. Bodies of Dan and Steve seen; body of Joe recovered.
	Martin Cherry removed from inn and dies a short time later.
Evening	Ned taken by train to Benalla
	Wake for Dan and Steve at Greta

MONDAY 29 JUNE

12.30 am	Johnny Jones dies at Wangaratta

1
A FOUNDATION MYTH

'Contact with the Kelly Gang'

On a bright but blustery day in May 2008, a battered green Land Rover eased to a halt at an unremarkable vacant block in a small town in north-eastern Victoria. At the wheel was a thirty-eight-year-old Englishman named Adam Ford. He was there to meet local media and show them a vacant lot—a long and somewhat tangled strip of trees, vines and rubble contained within an ordinary farm fence. Ford was an archaeologist who had worked in Europe, the Middle East and Australia. It was his hope, and the hope of many others, that the narrow corner block could reveal more about one of the most defining events in Australian history. The town was Glenrowan and the overgrown field was the site of the Glenrowan Inn, where Ned Kelly fought his Last Stand. Adam Ford was there to dig it up.

Ford had been given the formidable task of conducting the first-ever scientific excavation of the bush pub where the Kelly Gang took a town hostage and declared war on the government.

When the Last Stand was over, five people were dead, including a child, and the pub had burnt to the ground. But even as the ruins smouldered, the inn became the heart of a story that would fascinate, infuriate and delight Australians for generations. The site was burnt again, repeatedly looted and redeveloped before finally—a century after the first settlers built there—it was sealed off from development and disturbance. Adam Ford and a team of archaeologists were about to sift through it layer by layer, in the hope of getting back to its very beginnings.

Not only an experienced archaeologist, Ford was also a natural communicator with a lively sense of humour and an ability to translate complex scientific data into language that anyone could understand. These were useful skills because the work he was about to do at the Glenrowan Inn would attract more interest and debate than perhaps any other archaeological project in Australian history. Although he did not say so at the time, he was worried about the risk of failure. There was no way of telling what lay beneath the ground—if anything—and when it came to public expectations he was taking a professional gamble that could do a service to science and history, or collapse into irrelevance.

The Wangaratta Council had appointed Ford to lead the dig as part of their plans to establish the siege precinct as a more substantial tourist destination. Under a grandly named marketing plan to make the town the 'Keeping Place of the Kelly Legend', the council hoped to develop a Kelly interpretive centre of national significance. There was no definite proposal for the future of the privately owned inn site, but it was felt that the archaeological survey would provide some of the data needed to make the right decision.

Adam Ford. Image courtesy of Reece Rayner and Neal Kelly.

Ford had cut his archaeological teeth on ancient historical sites and like many archaeologists from the Old World he was never particularly interested in Australia. As a student in London, Ford had briefly thought of digging in Australia but concluded it would be 'like a tree surgeon moving to the Sahara'. After meeting an Australian girl in the United Kingdom, marrying and moving to Victoria to raise a family, however, he gained a better understanding of what Australia could offer a young archaeologist. Ford was aware that humans had occupied the land for at least 40,000 years and soon came to understand that, while Australia's colonial history was relatively short, it was just as colourful as that of older countries. Based at Ocean Grove on Victoria's south-west coast, he was building up a successful business called Dig International. Like many Englishmen, he was already well aware of the Kelly story and, when the chance came to excavate the Glenrowan site, he seized it with delight.

He had briefly wondered whether some Australians might resent an Englishman digging up this 'holy' place but he need not have worried. It has been a long time since the English were regarded with mistrust in Kelly Country.

The archaeological team was there to search for new evidence of those thirty-six turbulent hours in and around the tiny pub. The dig would seek physical and historical remains of the pub in the hope of reconstructing the gunbattle and learning more about what went on there as the fighting raged. And with the help of the Kelly scholars Ian Jones and Alex McDermott, the archaeologists would find new insights into the lives of ordinary people caught up in an extraordinary moment.

Jones had been studying the Kelly story for more than sixty years and had a forensic knowledge of its details, both great and small. He would use this knowledge to link discoveries from the site to the historical events, bringing alive the people who were there. McDermott was the official dig historian, a slightly controversial choice given his revisionist approach to Kelly history. McDermott would provide an insight into the life and times of Victoria during the Kelly years and a counterpoint to rethink some of the accepted versions of the story. The historians and archaeologists would be supported by descendants of the Kellys, their hostages and the police. They would provide family lore and local history to add a personal dimension to the investigation. Over the course of a month, the site of the Kelly Gang's Last Stand would be stripped bare, revealing a very human story of both heroism and frailty.

Peter Clifford, Tony Robinson, Ian Jones and Alex McDermott, Ned Kelly Uncovered. *Image courtesy of Renegade Films.*

When Ned Kelly and his gang held Glenrowan hostage in June 1880, they were committing more than a crime. They were trying to start an uprising, perhaps even a full-blooded revolution, to create a republic of north-eastern Victoria. It was grandly ambitious and doomed to fail but it rode on a wave of support from a horde of poor and oppressed sympathisers clamouring for change. It is not known exactly how many sympathisers there were but they were numerous enough, and discontented enough, to fuel a movement for reform with twenty-five-year-old Ned at its head. And Ned—famously clad in iron armour—eventually did play a part in bringing a fairer go to the masses. Along the way he helped to define what it means to be Australian. For Ned, however, the victory was a Pyrrhic one.

The Kellys were already a sensation when they came to Glenrowan on the cold winter's night of 26 June 1880. It had been just twenty spectacular months since they had slain three policemen at Stringybark Creek and now Ned, his nineteen-year-old brother Dan, Joe Byrne, twenty-three, and Steve Hart, twenty, were the most wanted men in the land. The deaths of the three policemen had launched the Kelly outbreak. Outlawed, with prices on their heads, the Kellys were striking back in what they believed was a legitimate war against oppression. Like the striking miners at Eureka twenty-five years earlier and the diggers at Gallipoli thirty-five years later, the Kelly Gang's final battle would form a foundation myth for the new nation.

The town of Glenrowan has kept very little of the landscape that made it part of the myth. None of the buildings that were there in 1880 have survived in their original locations. Some were demolished or burnt down and others were relocated or recycled into newer buildings. As a result, Glenrowan is a town with a rich history but little to show for it in a physical sense. The topography has not changed, though. The rail line from Melbourne still climbs a long path up to the town before cresting a rise and curving away steeply downhill to the north. It was because of the rail line—in particular that high point on the track just out of town—that Ned Kelly fought his Last Stand there.

For countless generations the area was home to the Yorta Yorta people. In the 1840s, Scottish brothers James and George Rowen took up a pastoral run there and adopted its Yorta Yorta name, 'Peechelba'. But by the 1870s, the town was known as Glenrowan. It boasted a schoolhouse and a police barracks, as well as the railway station and a scattering of houses along the gravel streets. It was a stopover point for Cobb & Co coaches for a time but it was the arrival of the rail line in 1874 that opened up new opportunities for growth. Foreseeing the changes that rail would bring, Ann Jones built her pub on the northern side of the tracks in the summer of 1878–79. The kitchen and residence behind the inn had been built about two years earlier. At the foot of a steep conical hill and surrounded by straggly eucalypts, Ann's hotel stood close enough to the station to catch passengers alighting and departing. On the other side of the rails, even more isolated in the rough scrub, was McDonnell's Hotel—an Irishman's pub and a stronghold for the Kellys and their friends. Although they sometimes shared the same customers—'mostly the working sort'—Ann liked to think her pub was more refined.

Visitors to Glenrowan today arrive to find a town that knows not only where its bread and butter come from, but also its jam and cream. Now with a population approaching a thousand, the locals are proud of their community and the Kelly story is genuinely celebrated. There was a time when invasive questioning might have earned you a punch in the nose in Glenrowan but those days are gone and the people are now friendly and welcoming. Today, Ned Kelly is good for business. In Glenrowan you can buy a Ned pie, a stuffed Ned, a painting of Ned, Ned on a mirror or Ned soap on a rope. There are Kelly Gang tea towels, stubby holders, T-shirts, calendars, books and movies. There are Ned pens, Ned posters and Ned key rings. And, of course, there are suits of armour. They range from plastic trinkets to tin reproductions small enough to carry in one hand to solid steel copies of the real thing. There are suits for all tastes; they even come in pastel pink. In the main street, speakers play ballads of Ned's war with the law and an animated theatre re-enacts the siege, on the half-hour, complete with tinny gunshots. You can be in no doubt as to this town's claim to fame.

In the best Australian tradition, there's even a Big Ned. Six metres tall and authentically clad in raincoat and armour, this fibreglass Ned clutches his revolving rifle and watches over the main street as buses disgorge throngs of tourists. They snap up the books and postcards, tea towels and trinkets—all emblazoned with images of the iconic outlaws. Few of the souvenirs celebrate the police who fought Ned to a standstill, nor the judge who sent him to the gallows. It says much about the marketability of Ned Kelly as an icon.

One of the town's main visitor drawcards is the animated theatre whose recorded gunshots provide the soundtrack for the passing tourist trade. A sign on the outer wall ominously warns, 'This attraction can and does frighten people of all ages!' Inside, the viewer walks from scene to scene, starting with the hunt for the Kellys amid a Halloween setting of giant spiders, snakes and a huge pumpkin. The next scene is the Glenrowan Inn, where Ned issues a call to arms, a drunk sleeps in a chandelier and someone is trying to escape from a cellar. Ann stands silently at the bar while rats scurry about and two dogs sit at a table with a small boy. Then the gang and police shoot it out— at a cemetery—and visitors re-enter the burning hotel before passing through the Old Melbourne Gaol where Ned meets his end. Things go crash and bang, lights flash and gunfire crackles. It is pantomime fun that entertains the kids, but if you are looking for an authentic insight into the Glenrowan siege then the town's theatre is not the place you need.

You can get a look inside the life of Glenrowan in 1880 thanks to two museums, Kate's Cottage and the Cobb & Co Museum. Named for Ned's sister, Kate's Cottage includes a convincing replica of the Kelly family homestead at Greta. It has a rustic, rugged kitchen and three small bedrooms. It gives an idea of some of the hardships faced by people who lived in homes just like it. A cabinet in the kitchen once belonged to Kate and a wooden trunk in a bedroom was owned by Ned's brother Jim. There is also a museum with artefacts, press reports and photographs. You can find similar relics a few doors away at the Cobb & Co Museum. Owned by local Kelly researcher and author Gary Dean, the museum is in the basement of a shop that sells souvenirs and trinkets. Downstairs there is replica armour, photos, documents and some artefacts from the old town of Greta. The museum also has a Ned death mask and some meticulous research on family trees, as well as original press reports and weaponry with reputed links to the Kelly outbreak.

In a geographical sense, the outbreak was a very Victorian story. Most of the action took place in a wedge of mountains, hills and plains that would become known as 'Kelly Country'. But people come to Glenrowan from all points. Schoolteachers from Sydney, painters from Perth or doctors from Darwin, they all share the heritage that Ned left in the town in 1880. After they have eaten or shopped, the tourists usually find their way across the railway bridge and down to the long, narrow block of land on its quiet street corner. There is not much to see—just the strip of dirt and grass, bordered on three sides by roads, and by a house with incongruous tropical trees and ferns on the fourth. Until the dig took place, the paddock was home to a small pony, a historically important fig tree and a huge peppercorn tree, some forty years old. The peppercorn tree is now gone but the pony has returned after a lengthy absence and the fig is still there. Totem figures of bushrangers stand at the front fence and a sign reveals the empty field to be the site of the Glenrowan Inn. The visitors take a moment to gaze at this vacant block, contained by its ordinary wire fence. As they look, those with good imaginations might close their eyes and sense the gunshots and screams echoing through the years. Others might shrug and ask: Is this all there is?

Diagonally opposite the vacant block is a flat piece of land leading to a replica of the original train station. This is the railway reserve, once a battleground studded with gum trees and scored with creeks and ditches. It was here that the police first laid siege to the inn, sheltering in the ditches and behind the trees as the Kelly bullets whistled overhead. But in June 2006, the battleground was lost. In a decision described by the Kelly historian Ian Jones as an 'act of historical vandalism' the reserve was bulldozed, the ditches concreted and the battlefield replaced by native shrubs and ordered rose gardens. It is neat and tidy but somehow inappropriate. The story of the Last Stand was anything but neat, and definitely not tidy.

Jones is the author of the definitive biography, *Ned Kelly: A Short Life*, and the producer of the television mini-series, *The Last Outlaw*. He had spent a lifetime examining minute details about the Kelly Gang and was thrilled at the chance to learn more about the siege. He hoped Ford's archaeological excavation would make up for some of the damage to the site. For him, the dig was also:

> a chance to make contact with the Kelly Gang and God knows we've lost contact with it at Glenrowan as it is now. I used to be able to walk around Glenrowan and feel what had happened there. I can't now. It would be wonderful to regain contact with the lives and deaths of members of the Kelly Gang.

Re-establishing those lost links would not be easy. The Kellys were only in Glenrowan for a few days and it was hard to say whether they left anything behind that could give any new clues to their actions before and during the siege. On the other hand, their time at the inn was both violent and momentous, and there were reasonable hopes that traces of what happened there might somehow have escaped the effects of time, looting and fire. If those traces existed it was Adam Ford's job to find them.

A search for what the inn site might reveal. Courtesy Reece Rayner and Neal Kelly.

2
KELLY COUNTRY

'Everyone looks on me like a black snake.'

We would never have heard of Ned Kelly had he not chosen to fight back. He'd grown up with tales of English oppression of the Irish, and was taught the memories of countless Irish peasants crushed under English boot heels and of Irish rebels who had paid with their lives. The old hatreds had been brought—literally in chains—to Australia and now the convicts and their native-born offspring could expect more of the same. But Ned Kelly was no ordinary native-born lad, and when he stood up to say 'Enough!' he spoke not only for himself but also for people who were crying out for change.

Ned never denied taking the lives of the policemen Michael Kennedy, Michael Scanlan and Thomas Lonigan at Stringybark Creek but always claimed it was in self-defence. For those killings, he claimed his right to a fair trial, got an unfair one, and was hanged with unseemly haste. When the executioner—a convicted chicken thief with the splendidly Dickensian name of Elijah Upjohn—placed the noose around Ned's neck, thousands of people had clamoured for his reprieve. It was clear that, whatever he had done, Ned Kelly was much more than a common criminal.

He was handsome, brave, strong and loyal. He was as tough as teak with a gentlemanly sense of honour. He was a crack shot, an expert horseman—and at heart, an Irish rebel. He was also a killer and bank robber. But he always believed he was fighting for the good of his family and community. For twenty months he roamed Kelly Country inspiring hope, fear and awe. Driven into a corner, he shouted his rage at the authorities but when they would not listen he went to war.

Ned Kelly the day before he was hanged, 1880.
Image courtesy of the Pictures Collection, State Library of Victoria.

Kelly Country is an inverted triangular wedge of north-eastern Victoria. Its apex points to Melbourne and its base blurs over the Murray River into southern New South Wales. The eastern side of the triangle follows the edges of the Victorian alps and the third side cuts through the broad farmland of the state's north. Glenrowan sits high in the upside-down triangle, some 200 kilometres north-east of Melbourne. It is now an easy few hours' freeway drive from the capital to the town and travellers can breeze through, barely disrupting their journey.

The country is crossed with a network of rivers and creeks that hurry down from the alps to join the Murray. To the west, the land flattens out into broad farmlands on the floors of the river valleys. To the east, the plains rise to steep wooded hills and rocky outcrops. The hills quickly give way to the mountains where the river valleys open out like fingers from a hand. Now there are towns, cities, freeways and factories but in Ned Kelly's time the country was a turbulent frontier where tough, clannish settlers battled the authorities, the elements and sometimes each other. With telegraph and rail still to complete their conquest of the bush, Kelly Country in 1880 remained a steep and secluded place where, with the help of friends, an outlaw could hide in safety.

There have been suggestions that support for the gang has been overstated but the fact that the Kellys could roam this semi-wild country with apparent immunity shows how deeply they were connected to their community, either through loyalty or fear. Their twenty months on the run captured a public imagination that was both outraged and thrilled. The press railed against the outlaws, and 'decent' folk—especially those in well-to-do areas of the cities—were suitably appalled at the gang's 'bloodthirsty outrages'. In the country and urban slums, though, there was a burning sympathy for the gang. It was a time when the tiniest spark could ignite angry men, and there were lots of angry men in the north-east as the 1870s drew to an end.

It was the men who did the fighting, with fists and guns, but the women fought wars too—battles of attrition against poverty, hardship and strife. Mothers, sisters, friends and lovers, they underpinned a movement for change, a growing demand for fairness and the right to raise a family in safety. The Kelly women were central to Ned's cause. The unjust imprisonment of his mother fuelled the anger that drove him and the epic horseback adventures of his sisters became part of the mythology.

Ann Jones, from The Cookson Series, *1911.*

Of all the women who defined the course of the Kelly out-break, Ann Jones would be one of the most influential but least remembered. Had it not been for a serious mistake by Ann, the Last Stand may never have happened. She was a victim of the siege but also of her own failings. Like a river diverted by a fallen log, history can change course in an instant and when Ned Kelly came to Glenrowan in June 1880, Ann's actions helped to decide that course. Fighting for her children and livelihood she had to choose a side. She took a chance. It left her with a lifetime of regret, and it helped to create the legend of Ned Kelly's Last Stand.

Ned Kelly's critics will say, quite correctly, that he was a criminal. So was his father, so were his cousins and so were his friends. Ned was a brilliant bushman who was very good with horses. He was especially good at stealing them. He was a key operative in a racket that might today be compared to the theft and rebirthing of cars in city suburbs. In a time and place where horses and cattle were the currency of success, Ned by his own admission was in the business of 'wholesale and retail' cattle and horse stealing.

Like many Australians of his time, Ned was literally born into the criminal class. He was the son of an Irish convict, John 'Red' Kelly. For stealing two pigs, Red was taken from his home at Tipperary and sent to the island prison of Van Diemen's Land on the other side of the world. He was released in January 1848 and sailed to the new colony of Victoria. In the spring of 1850, he eloped with Ellen Quinn—a member of another wild Irish clan with questionable regard for the law—and the young couple began a new life together.

Red and Ellen made their first home in a hut at Wallan, north of Melbourne, where their first child—a girl—was born. Mary Jane Kelly died in infancy but by late 1853 the couple's second daughter, Ann, arrived safely. The young family soon moved to the bush settlement of Beveridge on the windswept southern skirts of the Great Divide, and in another hut—on the side of a towering volcanic cone known as Big Hill—Ellen delivered the couple's first son. There is no reliable record of his birth date but it was probably in December 1854. They named him Edward.

Things seemed to be looking up for the family and with more children in mind they built a new, more substantial home not far from the town. That house still stands. Made of split palings with a shingled roof and a bluestone chimney, it defied hardship to survive, much like the family who built it. Over the next eleven years another five children were born: Margaret, James, Daniel, Catherine and Grace. They were baptised into the Catholic Church, given basic schooling and taught the rural skills they would need for everyday life in their hard world. They were a close family and the bonds between mother and children were particularly strong. Like so many of their type, the Kellys did it tough—just another battling family of Irish peasants transplanted to a new land. Just like any other family, that is, except for their oldest son.

Ned first made his mark when at the age of about eleven he dived into the flooded Hughes Creek at Avenel to rescue a younger boy, Richard Shelton, who was drowning in the rushing brown water. Both boys could have died but Ned saved young Richard and himself. The Shelton family was so grateful they presented Ned with a striking green waist sash, fringed with gold threads. Not even into his teens, Ned had earned hero status for the first time and he would be wearing that green sash as a symbol of his cause when he fell to his knees fifteen years later.

The rescue of Richard Shelton in 1865 was a bright spot in an otherwise bleak period for the Kelly family. In May that year Red was locked up for four months for possessing a stolen cow hide, leaving Ned and Ellen to shoulder the burden of running the failing family farm. By now Red was a heavy drinker, which probably contributed to a series of financial setbacks for his family. His alcohol abuse worsened after his release and his body steadily deteriorated over the next year. Two days after Christmas 1866, Red Kelly died of dropsy. Ned was now the man of the house; one of seven children in a home without a father or breadwinner. Soon the family would begin a new life in the north-east. Needing to be closer to the Quinn family in the isolated King Valley, the widow and her children moved to Greta, where they began to put down the roots that would one day define the region as Kelly Country.

But the poverty there was no better and the system just as harsh. Many of the children of convicts had little choice but to turn to crime to survive. Stock stealing was rampant and disputes were often settled in an arbitrary and bloody fashion. In February 1869, at the age of fifteen, Ned formally took to a life of crime when he was 'apprenticed' to the escaped bushranger Harry Power. Their exploits together were brief but dramatic, lasting less than eighteen months. Harry was captured in June 1870 while Ned was acquitted of robbery under arms a few weeks later. A letter that Ned wrote at around this time gives an insight into his sense of persecution. It was the first of several letters that defined the milestones of his life and it is the only one written in his hand to survive. It may also have been his most truthful. In it, a sad and frightened Ned wrote, 'everyone looks on me like a black snake'. His later letters would be much more strident.

He celebrated his sixteenth birthday in prison. In November, just five months after his acquittal of the robbery charge, Ned was sentenced to six months in Beechworth Gaol for assault—a matter for which he may have been wrongly convicted. In the years after his release he had a series of violent run-ins with police. Early in the spring of 1877, he became involved in a savage brawl with four police in the streets of Benalla. During the violent four-on-one arrest, Ned is said to have roared a famous death threat to Constable Thomas Lonigan. It was a fatal prophecy that came true the following year.

But it was when the drunken and corrupt Constable Alexander Fitzpatrick burst into the Kellys' family home that Ned's career in crime took an irreversible turn. In the so-called 'Fitzpatrick Incident', Ellen Kelly hit the wayward constable on the head with a fire shovel. It was that brief but violent confrontation in April 1878 that sent Ellen to gaol for attempted murder, and Ned and Dan into hiding in the rugged Wombat Ranges near Mansfield. Soon the brothers were joined by their mates Joe Byrne and Steve Hart and it was there, at Stringybark Creek, that they killed three of the four police officers sent to find them. The gunshots that rang out in the bush that day launched the Kelly outbreak.

In the months after the Stringybark Creek killings, the Kellys carried out dramatic bank robberies at Euroa and Jerilderie. They were dashing affairs, where dozens of people were bailed up and whole towns became part of the drama. The second robbery gave us Ned's greatest letter—a manifesto that became known as the Jerilderie Letter. The raids established not only Ned's generalship but also his reputation, as he charmed his victims, enthralled the press and enraged his enemies. He shared the proceeds with his poverty-stricken friends and he led the authorities on a futile chase through Kelly Country. He was hated, feared, admired and revered. He was already becoming a romantic bandit out of the pages of a history book—a real-life Robin Hood.

It's also true, however, that Ned Kelly was a crook, and after Stringybark Creek he had blood on his hands. And his plan for the uprising at Glenrowan was horrifying. Backed into a corner, he was plotting the mass murder of two dozen people in a train crash and with it a call to take up arms against the government. Today, we still argue whether the plan was a declaration of war or a terrorist plot.

Yet he was a man who spoke for a people with a legitimate grievance. These people were an underclass, grimly poor and deliberately kept that way. They were harassed by a police force that was often corrupt and in the service of rich men—the politicians, the lawyers, the squatters and the colonial government of the British Crown. The gold rush had made the rich men even richer and brought boom times to the colony. Now the rush was over and the land was being opened for agriculture but the best went to squatters and other men of money while the poor farmed stumps and rocks and lived in huts of bark and wood. When Ned Kelly found himself driven from society, his family dishonoured and his mother unfairly slung in gaol, he took a stand.

Ned was the last of the bushrangers and among the last of the world's highwaymen. Even in America the days of the outlaw gunslinger were drawing to a close. The Wild West gunmen Jesse James and Billy the Kid would outlive Ned Kelly by just a year or two, ending a similar chapter in American history. All three outlaws would go down in history, but unlike Jesse and Billy, Ned would be remembered as more than just a bandit with a six-gun and a willingness to use it. When Ned took up arms for the gunfight at the Glenrowan Inn he did it in such a remarkable way that future generations could never truly define him.

3

BENEATH THE SIEGE

'My poor, innocent children!'

The owner of the inn site, local man and lifelong beekeeper and cattle producer Linton Briggs, believes Kelly artefacts are hidden in homes, sheds and attics across Australia, particularly in the north-east, and that some of them may yet come to light. Briggs hoped the dig would lead to the development of an interpretive centre in Glenrowan—a place where people could visit to feel the story come alive and where hidden relics of the Kelly Gang could finally be shared with the public. He will not say where he thinks the relics are, but he is sure they are in the hands of people who would share them if the museum is built.

The narrow corner block has been in the Briggs family for more than fifty years. Linton's father, John, bought it when the last building on the site—a tavern known as 'the wine shanty'—was still standing. The shanty later became a café, then a hair salon, and finally it was converted into two flats. The Briggs family demolished it in 1976 when rising damp became a problem.

When he was a boy, Linton Briggs knew Ned Kelly's sister Grace (Griffiths) and Ned's brother Jim 'quite well'. Briggs was a close friend of Grace's sons—Ned's nephews—and was mindful of the importance of the site to them and other local people. When the wine shanty was demolished, Briggs decided not to build on the empty block, which has since been placed on the Heritage Register, but he has many ideas to revitalise Glenrowan as a leading tourist attraction and believed the archaeological survey of the inn site would be an important step.

Adam Ford gazed at the site for what seemed like the hundredth time. He was looking at a long, narrow lot 24 metres wide and 85 metres long. The land rose steadily towards the back fence on a north–south axis, and at some stage in the twentieth century a low concrete terrace had been built about a quarter of the way into the block. There were concrete slabs on the ground at the base of the terrace. The terrace and the slabs were associated with the wine shanty and, sadly for the archaeologists, they had probably been cut directly into the back of Ann Jones' inn.

The peppercorn tree dominated the front of the field. The tree had been planted (probably right on top of Ann's bar room) soon after the demolition of the wine shanty in 1976. Now its roots must surely have wrapped themselves tightly around any remnants of the inn or siege, and to tear them out would be devastating to the archaeology. It was felt, however, that the roots would otherwise have caused little damage and it would be safe, if somewhat inconvenient, to dig between them. The tree would have to come down but the broad, flat stump and its web of roots would remain.

Elevated view of the dig showing the shanty foundations. Siege Street at right. Image courtesy of Reece Rayner and Neal Kelly.

There was a tangle of undergrowth between the tree and the neighbour's iron fence along the eastern side. This mess of brambles and vines was not deep-rooted enough to cause any serious problems and would be easily removed. A large wooden sign stood at the front of the lot. This was an authentic replica of the original Glenrowan Inn sign. Linton Briggs had reproduced it from the only photographs taken of the inn and erected it where the original had stood in the winter of 1880. The replica sign was carefully removed for the dig.

To the north, beyond the concrete terrace, the block was clear all the way to the back fence, except for a small fig tree in a wire cage. This was a tree with a pedigree. Ann Jones had planted its parent behind her residence in the 1870s. It survived the siege and fire, living for more than a century, until the summer of 1997–98, when it succumbed to a combination of drought and ringbarking by a horse. It was chopped down but its stump sent up a sucker and Linton Briggs enclosed it in a wire cage. It was now growing slowly but surely. The little fig tree in its protective cage was the empty block's only living link to Ann Jones.

There had been less construction activity on the back half of the block and the archaeology there might have been less disturbed. Ann's stables had been at the rear, in the north-eastern corner. If time permitted, a small dig could establish their precise location and probably turn up some valuable arte-facts. There was also a hope that the inn's cesspits—or rubbish dumps—would be found. Filled with the daily refuse of life in a busy nineteenth-century pub, these pits would be difficult to locate but would surely be something of an archaeological treasure trove if found.

The first target of the dig was the inn itself. The second target was Ann's kitchen and home at the rear of the inn. The residence had been the first building on the site and, as a fam-ily home that doubled as an industrial kitchen and laundry, it would probably contain valuable evidence of the way Ann lived and worked. The residence would be excavated if time permit-ted but the dig was budgeted for only twenty-eight days and most of the team had commitments to other jobs when it was completed. It was not expected to be a straightforward excava-tion and it could take the whole month just to find the inn and its contents. That is if they were even there.

On the plus side, Adam Ford had had a head start, having dug small exploratory trenches during a visit a few months ear-lier. He had cut one trench into a small section of what is now the footpath in Siege Street, directly in front of where the inn's verandah would have stood. It had paid off immediately with the discovery of a small brass tube, about the size of a man's thumb. This was a cartridge from a Martini-Henry rifle, the main weapon used by police in colonial times, and it may well have been associated with the gunfight.

After more than a century below the ground, the shell was crusted with dirt but was otherwise remarkably intact. The last man to have held it was a policeman and he may very well have fired it at the Kelly Gang. It was an excellent thing to find even before the dig started but it was also a reminder of the martial nature of this site. Hundreds of shots had been fired into a small hotel filled with terrified hostages. People died violently here and, although generations had passed, Adam Ford knew it would be a sensitive dig under intense scrutiny.

The first job was to clear the vegetation, starting with the peppercorn tree. Council workers moved in with trucks, power saws and chippers, and dismantled the old tree from the top down. Soon it was a pile of severed limbs and then, after being fed through a shredder, it was no more than a truckload of woodchips. The archaeologists did not like this tree and there was some satisfaction at its demise. As the tree came down, a second council crew built a viewing platform with signage at the western side of the site, along Beaconsfield Parade. Lots of visitors were expected and the platform would provide a safe and elevated viewing point. In the end, it was well used. As the dig progressed, waves of visitors mounted the platform or leaned on the fences to watch the team at work.

Students from La Trobe University in Melbourne were brought in to help. Under a training program overseen by the university's executive dean of archaeology, Professor Tim Murray, the students arrived in rotating groups of about a dozen a week, enthusiastic and thrilled to have a chance to work on this site. What they lacked in experience they made up for in hard work and a willingness to learn. There was also a stream of volunteers—mostly long-time Kelly enthusiasts who were more than happy to swing a pick or shovel at the place where the story climaxed. Ford's core team consisted of six experienced archaeologists. Second in charge was the veteran archaeologist and former British soldier Jon Sterenberg. The field archaeologists were Cosmos Coroneos, Natalie Paynter and Caroline Wilby. Fenella Atkinson was the finds officer and the dig conservator, Karina Acton, was to treat any artefacts found below the soil.

Archaeologists at work. Ash marks show inn ruins. Image courtesy of Reece Rayner and Neal Kelly.

Once the vegetation was gone, metal detection expert Bob Sheppard surveyed the entire block. Within an hour he had recorded hundreds of strikes and marked them with tiny grey flags. Soon the block was a sea of markers, each denoting a buried metallic mystery. Sheppard could tell the depth of each object, and although most would prove to be twentieth-century junk (copper coins, car parts, scraps of wire, bottle tops), some were deep enough and in the right location to point to finds relating directly to the hotel or the siege.

As the work progressed, Adam Ford again wondered briefly if the dig might fail but put the thought to one side. The project had defined targets and all he could do was try to reach them:

> The priority is to find the physical remains of the siege, including the burnt remains of the building and, of course, the projectiles and cartridges from the battle, and so we're going to approach it as a conflict site. But even just the small personal items like cups and saucers and glasses will give us a personalised level to the story and hopefully we'll find lots of those as well.

The search for personal evidence would focus on Ann Jones and her family. Ford saw the dig as a chance to learn more about the life of a woman who should be better known to all Australians. He saw Ann as a strong character who had been overshadowed by the Kelly Gang and he hoped the dig would unearth new information about her and her family. Ford also hoped to examine some of the myths behind the legend, including the rumours that Dan Kelly and Steve Hart survived the siege. Part of the answer to that question lay in establishing whether a fabled cellar existed beneath the inn. If there was a cellar, then one of the most enduring myths about the Last Stand would gain new impetus.

Adam Ford was keeping an open mind on the cellar theory but he was certain of one thing. 'You can't hide a hole in the ground,' he said. 'If there was a cellar below the pub, we'll find it. Whether that solves the mystery is another question entirely.'

By the end of the first day of digging, Ann Jones' long, narrow field looked like a construction site. Piles of spoil were rising around the edges as the students carried dirt to one side where it was sifted for anything of value. The early digging was done by hand and the dirt flew as young people in safety vests shifted earth at an astonishing rate. A bright orange safety fence now ringed the field and a small green tent had gone up next to the neighbour's fence. Onlookers began to gather on the viewing platform and at the fences to watch a squadron of people dig, sift, measure and record. A large, square hole in the ground at the front of a weedy, vacant block had become a tourist attraction.

But on the second day, an important discovery quickly made it clear that this trench was much more than just a hole in the ground. When patient trowel work uncovered a thin disc of lead about the size of a fingernail, Adam Ford knew he had found what he was looking for. The little sliver of dull, grey metal did not look much to the untrained eye but to Adam Ford and Jon Ster-enberg, an ex-soldier, it was paydirt. They realised immediately that they had found one of the hundreds of lead balls that had been fired into the pub during the siege. Flattened on impact with the building or perhaps even a suit of armour, the spent slug—or 'splat'—had escaped countless souvenir hunters for 128 years.

This was a sensational find that meant the dig had already achieved one aim—to find physical remains of the battle. Even better, now there was reason to think that more bullets would be found. It was an exciting start, but with hindsight perhaps not as surprising as it might have seemed. So many bullets were fired into the hotel that even generations of scavengers could not find them all. In any case, now there was conclusive evidence of incoming ballistics and for a moment Ford dared to dream that the inn could yield evidence of outgoing fire as well—proof of activity by the gang. If that evidence existed, however, it would be at the very bottom of the site and there were a range of hurdles to leap first.

For one thing, the team was looking for traces of a wooden building that stood for less than two years before burning down. Its signature in time and place was brief and might have left little physical evidence. And if that was not challenging enough, the archaeologists also had to consider the construction and demolition of three other buildings on the site, one on top of the other.

The rebuilding started soon after the siege when Ann Jones built a rough hut against the ruins of the parlour chimney. This second building, rude as it was, would have left a trace in the ground. Then, when Ann won a small victory in a bitter fight for compensation, she erected a new pub directly over the remains of the first. Fifteen years later, it too burnt to the ground. This would have created an archaeological puzzle because it meant the ground contained the remains of three similar buildings, two of which were destroyed in the same way within just a few years of each other. The team would have to differentiate between them, if it could.

The fourth and final building would create perhaps the greatest challenge. This was the wine shanty, a square brick building of many rooms and measuring about 12 metres by 12 metres. It went up early in the new century, directly over the remains of the earlier three buildings and had stood there for more than sixty years, unremarkable except for its location. Then, when it was demolished in 1976, the narrow block was finally left empty after more than a century of constant occupation. So, before the first sod had been turned, the team had known that even if traces of Ann's hotel had survived, they could be mixed up in an almost incomprehensible swirl of occupation, construction and demolition.

And then there was human disturbance to consider. Surely no other vacant lot has been picked over as much as the site of Ann Jones' inn. Even as the ashes cooled from the fire in 1880, people were sifting through the ruins, carting off treasures great and small. A hostage at the siege, fifteen-year-old Thomas Cameron, was one of the first. In a letter to his brother soon after the Last Stand ended, he described the finds he had gathered from the ruins:

> I have a cross and a small shield made out of one bullet Ned Kelly fired off at the police and I have some small revolver cartridges that I found near where Dan Kelly and Steve Hart were burned, and I have some other things that I got there. I will send them down to you if you like and I know where I could get one of their rings too, they will be relics, you know.

Sixty years after the battle, another of the prisoners recalled similar looting. As an old man, John Lowe, a former gravel carter from Benalla, wrote down his memories of hordes of people sifting through the ruins for souvenirs. He noted that the public's fascination with the siege story was insatiable. Hours after the siege ended, young John received so many visitors desperate to hear his story that he fell asleep in a chair and his mother had to kick them out of the house. Decades had passed when he wrote his account but he could vividly recall crowds of people plundering the ruins for anything they could find:

> The number of people that came to see the place was enormous. On every train there was a lot. As many as 50, getting off, besides others that came by road. It was surprising to see the various things they would take away as momentos [*sic*]; bits of iron, saucepans, pots, dishes, pieces of half-burnt furniture, legs and sides of bedsteads etc.

John Lowe was also one of the first to notice the booming trade in Kelly souvenirs. He cut spent bullets ('and there was many of them') out of trees and got two shillings each. But supply fell as demand rose so an enterprising rail line repairer came up with a nice little earner. 'He had a single barrel gun,' wrote Lowe. 'He made bullets with a hammer ... fired them into a tree. He told me he got 1/6 for them easy.'

Almost everything that could be carried away was systematically removed until the field was bare, but for the two chimneys and the Glenrowan Inn sign. Pilfering continued on and off over the years. People came and went, picking at the site like crows at a carcase. Then, when metal detectors were invented, even more might have been lost to treasure hunters scouring the field under cover of darkness. All this had occurred on a block of land that had seen four construction phases, two fires and a hundred years of occupation—yet the archaeologists were searching for the site's very beginnings.

It seemed daunting—and it was—but there were also good reasons for optimism. For one thing, the site had never been scientifically excavated. Although there had been one small amateur dig around twenty years earlier, Ford thought the archaeological damage would be minimal. Apart from that one small incursion, professionals had never excavated the field. This could make all the difference. It would certainly mean that if there were anything left of the siege under the ground the archaeologists would find it.

And for another thing, the discovery of the cartridge and spent slug proved that at least some relics of the era had survived and there was a good chance of finding more. Further ballistics finds would do a lot to tell the story of the siege from the inside of the hotel while the confirmation that relics remained meant the team could be more optimistic about finding domestic bits and pieces of everyday life.

The records also provided clues that would help to narrow the search. It was known, for example, that the inn was made of timber and iron, and its foundations were unmilled wooden posts. It was also recorded that ten gallons of spirits were destroyed in the fire. Importantly for the archaeologists, the heat from a spirit-fuelled fire would have left a distinctive trace that should be possible to find. It could also be assumed that the floor had been made of milled pine boards supported by joists that sat directly on the earth, a common way of building at the time. Finally, there was a wealth of documentation about the inn—much of it provided by the media of the day. Journalists had always recorded the Kelly Gang's exploits and the reporters of the time produced some excellent material that would help Ford and his team more than a century later.

The train that delivered the police to Glenrowan on 28 June 1880 also carried reporters and an artist from Melbourne. They steamed into the scoop of a lifetime, making records that would underpin modern understanding of the site. Other journalists arrived from the nearby towns of Benalla and Wangaratta. In particular, photographer Oswald Madeley and reporter and artist Thomas Carrington captured images that would help to reveal more about the pub decades after its destruction.

Madeley arrived just in time to record history unfolding. Laboriously he loaded the new-fangled glass plates for his cumbersome camera on its heavy tripod and then, risking the bullets, he took images that would be pored over for generations. His photographs show a typical late nineteenth-century bush pub, bookended by brick chimneys with a broad verandah and six posts along the front. There are two doors and three windows—one each for the parlour, bar and dining room. A table stands on the verandah. It had been brought out from the dining room before the siege started to make way for a rather remarkable celebration.

In one shot, smoke is starting to waft from the hotel's western, parlour side. This was taken moments after the police set fire to the building. The rough slab home of the Jones family with its iron chimney can be seen just behind the pub. Within moments of Madeley clicking the shutter both buildings were consumed by flames. Importantly, Madeley's pictures showed exactly where the inn stood and what it looked like. They are also the only photographs ever taken of Ann Jones' humble home.

Jones' hotel before the fire, 1880. Roadworkers' tents at right. Photographer Oswald Madeley. Image courtesy of the Pictures Collection, State Library of Victoria.

No photos were taken inside the pub and there were no planning records when it was built but witness accounts give a good description of the layout. It is widely thought that there were five rooms. Along the front, a central bar room was flanked by a dining room to the east, and a small parlour to the west. At the rear were two bedrooms separated by a narrow passage. The passage ended at the back door, which opened onto a breezeway between the pub and Ann's home—a rudimentary building of timber slabs with a bark roof. It had two bedrooms and a large kitchen with a big iron fireplace on the eastern wall and might have had a stone floor. It was a crowded place for a family of six to live but the kitchen was warm and there was always food for the table.

While the shape and design of the inn were fairly well known before the dig, there was little to say what it was like inside. How was it furnished? Were there decorations? What did the people eat and drink? And what was it really like when the bullets began to punch through the wooden walls like needles through a cotton sheet? The archaeologists hoped to answer at least some of these questions. Ann's furnishings and decorations were blasted to pieces during the siege; glasses were shattered, ornaments were smashed, bottles were broken. If any of these scraps survived they would paint a picture of life inside Ann Jones' inn, right up to the drama that ended it.

The dig eventually uncovered an astonishing 11,000 artefacts, each giving a tiny glimpse of the lives of the countless people who lived, worked and played on this one little corner block. A handful of these artefacts could be linked directly to people who were there during the siege.

4
MURDER IN THE VALLEY

'This foul deed'

Ned Kelly might have been the last of the bushrangers but he was not the first, and Glenrowan was not unfamiliar with outlaws. The town is dominated by the cone-shaped Mount Glenrowan to the north, behind the inn block. Better known as Morgan's Lookout, this tree-covered outpost of the Warby Ranges was named after another colourful crook, Daniel 'Mad Dan' Morgan. As his nickname suggests, Morgan was not a model citizen. His story parallels Ned's in that it tells of a bushranger on the run, robbing people at gunpoint, killing police and ending in the outlaw's violent death. But Morgan had none of Ned's dash or chivalry. Mad Dan (later known as 'Mad Dog' after a movie was made about him in the 1970s) was shot dead near Wangaratta in 1865 and his head was removed. Some accounts of Morgan's death say his scrotum was also removed and made into a tobacco pouch.

It was said that Mad Dan used to climb the hill to watch for police and spy over the land. It is possible that Ned did the same.

If so, he would have seen a town straddling the gouge mark of the new rail line with a scattering of roads and buildings amid eucalypt scrub on both sides of the track. Ann's hotel was in the foreground, on the northern side, facing the railway reserve and track. The station stood to the south-east of the inn while a cluster of buildings, including Thomas Curnow's schoolhouse and Hugh Bracken's police barracks were several hundred metres away to the west. The stationmaster's house with its important railway gate hugged the rail line on the northern side of the tracks and on the southern side—almost directly opposite Ann's—was the hotel of Ned's friend Paddy McDonnell.

The original railway platform is still there but only small plaques remain to mark where the other buildings once stood. McDonnell's—which looked similar to Ann Jones' hotel from the front—was one of the last to go. It survived well into the twentieth century, and if it could have lasted just a few more years we might still have it today. It was pulled down in the 1960s to make way for a new motel. The motel ended up being built elsewhere and the McDonnell's site is now just an empty lot right next door to the town's only pub, the late Victorian-era Glenrowan Hotel. All that remains of the town's last original building from the Kelly uprising is a few photographs and some brickwork under the ground.

The high, curving arch of the road bridge over the railway line dominates the view towards town from the front of the inn site. The bridge has replaced the railway gate where horses and carts once crossed the tracks but it is not a thing of beauty and it has not done the site any aesthetic favours. Still, it does its job and you can cross it by foot or by car to get back onto the main street.

From there, you could turn left, pick up the freeway and head north to Sydney or turn right for Melbourne to the south. In 1880, there was another major route—the Goldfields Road that headed south-east over the flat-bottomed bowl of Greta before turning back to the north-east and then up on to the rocky plateau of the diggings around Beechworth. This bustling gold town was central to what happened at Glenrowan, because it was there, on the town's hard fringes, that the gang lit the fuse on the uprising. At a modest hut almost hidden in scrubby bushland, two shots rang out that would be echoed by hundreds more at the Glenrowan Inn.

Today's visitor can still follow the old route to the goldfields. The former highway is now a network of country roads that pass through the Greta district, the one-time home of the Kelly family. The traveller can detour down well-graded dirt roads to pass the site of the old Kelly family homestead—and many do. There are still remnants of the Kellys and their associates in and around Greta, and some of the people living there can trace their family histories back to the outbreak, but the township has vanished, leaving only a few earthworks to show where it stood. Like McDonnell's Hotel in Glenrowan, Greta's last original building—the old police station—survived well into the twentieth century before it was demolished. It was last used as a post office and, ironically, the tenants were Quinns—of the Quinn-Kelly clan.

Beyond Greta the road rises through a gap towards the table-land of Beechworth. The rocky ground here was once rich with gold. At its peak, a staggering 14,000 ounces of the precious metal were transported under armed guard to Melbourne every fortnight. Beechworth now claims to be one of Victoria's best-preserved gold rush towns, which is no idle boast. Thanks to an absence of 'development' last century and a powerful drive since to protect its heritage, the town's streetscape has survived remarkably intact. Many of the original buildings where the Kellys might have worked and shopped or even served prison time still stand. Except for the cars in the streets and the tourists on the footpaths, the visitor can easily picture Beechworth as it was in the winter of 1880.

Just to the north-west of the town the road descends sharply into the Woolshed Valley, once a series of brawling shanty towns of gold diggers, rogues and prostitutes. As the gold rush faded, the valley became home to communities of struggling settlers, including the Byrne family. Like Greta, the old towns in the valley have gone—but they have left their scars on the landscape if you know where to look. Once, the stony hills and slopes here were blasted clean by miners with pressure hoses. Others delved into the rock like ants. Now, the scrub has returned, masking hundreds of mine shafts in the hard ground. The shafts are still there—neat and square vertical tunnels dug by the practical European gold seekers, or smooth and round holes made by the industrious Chinese, who feared the corners of square tunnels would hide malign spirits. Some of the shafts have been filled in but others still descend deep into the ground. It is wise to stick to the marked trails in Beechworth's historic park. A careless walker could tumble into one of these dark pits. In June 1880, however, the danger came from somewhere very different.

As the Jones family worked at the inn on the evening of 26 June, two men leading a packhorse carrying a curious load made their way through the Woolshed Valley under the moon shadow of a high, craggy peak. The men were Joe Byrne—Ned's good mate—and Dan Kelly, Ned's nineteen-year-old brother. Their load included two sets of steel body armour. The Byrne family homestead was nearby, on the open country under the rocky peak, but it was dangerous for Joe to go there. He knew his home was under police surveillance and spies were everywhere. It was one such spy who had brought Joe back to the valley. His name was Aaron Sherritt and he had been Joe's lifelong friend.

Dan Kelly, circa 1876–78. Photographer James E. Bray.
Image courtesy of the Pictures Collection, State Library of Victoria.

Aaron—a Protestant—had grown up with Catholic Joe and the two had been friends since their childhood at the valley's Common School. Aaron was a tough, athletic man who had said that only Ned Kelly himself was harder. Aaron was also a good runner and jumper and was known to have slept outdoors in his shirtsleeves in the dead of winter. As a member of the 'Greta Mob', a group of wild young men with scant regard for the law, Aaron wore the larrikin uniform of high-heeled boots, a waist sash and a hat strap fastened under the nose. This marked him as a tough man and not one to be trifled with. He had had his share of trouble with the police and in 1876 had done prison time with Joe for cattle theft. Soon after his release, Aaron was charged with assaulting a Chinese miner during a fight in the Woolshed Valley. When Ned and Dan had first fled to the Wombat Ranges after the Fitzpatrick Incident, Aaron had joined them, living as one of the 'merry men' in the bush.

By the start of 1880, however, Aaron had become the bait in a trap. He attempted to play for both sides and paid the price. One of the detectives on the Kellys' trail, Michael Ward, had cooked up a scheme to smoke the gang out of hiding. The police approached Aaron with an offer to become a police agent in return for pay and a promise to spare Joe Byrne's life. Aaron signed on as a police informant and he showed them to a cave in the rocky crag overlooking the Byrne homestead, where the police could watch for signs of the gang. Aaron went to the cave with the police at night and during the day the troopers would rest inside his tiny two-roomed hut.

Detective Ward, meanwhile, let it be known that Aaron was an informer. Ward knew that word would leak to the gang and that they would have no choice but to break out and strike. It might mean that Aaron would die, but once the gang came out of hiding the police could swoop. Joe's mother saw Aaron with the police and his treachery was exposed. Joe was infuriated and he convinced Ned that Aaron must die. A traitor could not be tolerated. Ward's plan appeared to be working. The Kelly Gang would have to break out to kill Aaron Sherritt. But what the police did not know was that Ned had a plan of his own.

Six months earlier, Aaron had married fifteen-year-old Ellen (Belle) Barry and she was now carrying the couple's first child. They made their home in a small timber hut by the side of a narrow rutted road at a settlement called Sebastopol in the Woolshed Valley. Today, there's almost nothing to mark where the hut stood except for irises that bloom by the roadside each spring. These are said to be the remnants of the Sherritts' garden, perhaps planted by the child-bride Belle in the bright hope of a new life in her new home. Whatever hopes Belle had were literally blasted apart by a man who had been her husband's closest friend.

For his part, Joe Byrne was convinced that Aaron was a traitor. History recorded him that way, too. But it is possible that history—and Joe—both got it wrong. While there is no doubt that Aaron was a police spy, some historians now believe he might have been a double agent, happily accepting payment from the police while actually doing his best to keep them away from the gang. It is true that much of the information he gave the police was old or unreliable and that the hours of spying from the cave high on the craggy peak never led the police to Joe. And Aaron's insistence that Joe should not be killed when the gang was caught is well documented. But unfortunately for Aaron, if he really was a double agent he neglected to tell Joe.

Soon after nightfall on 26 June, Joe and Dan quietly led their horses along the bush road leading to the Sherritt home. Joe carried a shotgun the gang had stolen from the police at Stringybark Creek. Now he would use it to kill Aaron Sherritt—in the only undisputed cold-blooded murder committed by the Kelly Gang.

Aaron was now in fear of attack and Joe and Dan knew that he would be difficult to reach. As they crept closer to the hut, they found the opportunity they needed when they came across Anton Wick, a German market gardener and neighbour of Aaron's. Joe and Dan clamped handcuffs on Wick's wrists and forced him to approach the back door of the Sherritt home. Inside were Aaron and the pregnant Belle, as well as Belle's mother, Ellen Barry, and the four policemen, who were preparing for another cold night in their spies' cave.

When Wick knocked at the Sherritts' door, the policemen—Constables Armstrong, Alexander, Duross and Dowling—crowded into the bedroom and shut the door. Under orders from Joe, Wick called out that he had lost his way. Anton lived in a small hut surrounded by gardens and fruit trees less than a mile from the Sherritt house and it amused Aaron that his neighbour could be lost so close to home. When he opened the back door, Aaron saw a shadowy figure standing behind Wick. Aaron uttered his last words—'Who's that?'—and then Joe shot him twice, once in the throat and once in the lower body. In a spray of blood, Aaron collapsed to the floor in front of his horrified wife. The four police remained hidden in the bedroom during the entire ordeal.

The police superintendent, Francis Hare, later wrote that Aaron might have become a bushranger if he had lived and that his wife 'was much better off without him'. Belle Sherritt saw it quite differently. A year after the killing, she told *The Ovens and Murray Advertiser* how the violent death of her 'husband and protector' rendered her unable to work or even to continue living in the Woolshed Valley. She said she had been ill ever since the murder and 'at one period I had two doctors attending to me, owing to serious illness'. Belle was living on government support of ten shillings a week, just enough for rent and firewood. Soon after the shooting she lost her unborn baby. In 1884, she remarried and had two children but the trauma of her first husband's murder stayed with her for life.

The first stage of Ned's plan was complete. He knew that the murder would bring a trainload of police rushing from Melbourne to Beechworth to catch the gang and he was plotting a terrible surprise. He planned to uproot the rail line on the high curving crest at Glenrowan to destroy the train and everybody on board. The Kelly Gang's supporters would then rise up in a demand for justice. It was a crude plan for revolution, possibly with an equally unrefined plan to create a republic in the northeast, but as a violent political statement it just might have worked.

It was then, however, that things began to go wrong.

Instead of immediately rushing off to raise the alarm as Ned expected, the four police assigned to Aaron Sherritt remained hiding in the tiny bedroom. They refused Joe's orders to reveal themselves, even after shots were fired into the room. Despite pleas from Mrs Barry not to risk her daughter's life, Dan lit a small fire against the side of the hut, perhaps in the hope of smoking the troopers out of hiding. Even with the bloody body of her new husband lying on the floor, Belle could not persuade the constables to run for help. They later said they discussed rushing out of the bedroom for a gunfight with the bushrangers but deemed it too risky. Joe and Dan had done their job too well. The four police did not leave the hut until dawn—hours after the bushrangers had ridden away, the iron armour still strapped to the packhorse.

There was more bungling the next morning. When the police emerged into the dawn light they tried to send a message for help with a passing 'Chinaman'. The Chinese miner accepted the message but then wisely thought better of passing it on. It was not his fight. He returned the note to the hapless four. Joe's old school teacher Cornelius O'Donoghue then passed by and he agreed to take the message. The teacher, who was a supporter of the Kellys, returned a short time later saying his wife did not want him to get involved. Then a miner named Duckett said he would take the message but did not return. Eventually, Constable Armstrong went himself and word of the attack was finally sent to Melbourne at one o'clock in the afternoon, nineteen hours after Aaron's murder. A telegraph from Beechworth sent a shock wave through the colony.

Watch party stuck up by the Kelly Gang at 6 o'clock Saturday night. Aaron Sherritt shot dead in the hut he occupied by Joe Byrne. Fired seven shots into the hut, the bullets passing by the constables' heads; but owing to the position taken by the outlaws the constables could not return a single shot . . .

As Ned Kelly had planned, the news spread like wildfire and the newspapers did their part by quickly blaming the Kellys for the murder. *The Argus* reported:

The town was thrown into a state of great consternation to-day, upon the arrival of Constable Armstrong . . . with the report that a man named Aaron Sherritt had been shot dead at Sebastopol on the previous night. This report proved true, and the perpetrators of this foul deed are without doubt the Kelly Gang.

This was the message that Ned wanted sent to Melbourne. The problem was that it should have been sent much earlier. Ned had been planning on a fast response by the police but the timidity of the troopers in the hut meant his plot was already fatally delayed. A few hours after the shots rang out in the Woolshed Valley, Ned and Steve Hart arrived in Glenrowan, expecting a train to be dispatched directly into their trap. But as the hours ticked by the police remained unaware that the trap had been set and by the time they reacted, it would already have been sprung.

5
ANN JONES

'The fast track to success'

To understand the archaeology of a site it helps to know the people who occupied it. In the case of the Glenrowan Inn, we know that Ann Jones lived there with her five youngest children. They were fourteen-year-old Jane, or Jenny, and four boys, Johnny (Jack), thirteen, Owen, eleven, Jeremiah, seven, and little Heddington, who was not yet three. They lived a crowded but relatively happy existence in the kitchen and two bedrooms of their slab home with its pub at the front. It was a brand-new enterprise with plenty of promise following the recent arrival of the rail line.

Ann had already been caught up in the turmoil of the Kelly outbreak. She was under pressure from the police who were trying to use her to catch the gang. Detective Michael Ward, in particular, was keeping a close eye on Ann's pub in case the Kellys visited. At the same time, some of Ann's customers included the friends and families of the outlaws and many people in her community were fervent sympathisers. Ann did not want to alienate either side. The mistake she made was to sit on the fence. As a result, she pleased neither the police nor the Kelly supporters. The police now suspected her of harbouring the fugitives while the Kellys loathed her as a police spy. She was in a difficult position, partly of her own making.

On the morning of 27 June, however, her problems were closer to home. She was sick, suffering from 'neuralgia in my head' and had been so ill—or claimed to be—that she had been confined to her bed. One of her neighbours even thought she might be close to death but within hours she would make a remarkable recovery. Ill or not, Ann's spell in bed left fourteen-year-old Jane to shoulder much of the burden of running the pub. One of the first jobs of the day was to light the fires; first the cooking range in the kitchen and later the open fires in the parlour and dining room. In summer, Glenrowan bakes under a vast blue sky but in winter, frost cracks the ground and puddles harden into muddy chunks of ice. It was particularly cold in the last days of June 1880.

Johnny was a frail boy but at thirteen and the man of the house he had to do his share of the work. Ann and her Welsh-born husband, Owen, lived apart. He was working on the railways in Gippsland. Despite fathering eleven children with Ann, by 1880 he had little to do with his family and nothing to do with the running of the pub. Ann accepted money from Owen and returned to him for a short time after the siege but he played no part in his family's day-to-day life. They remained married until Owen's death but before that Ann was happy to be known as 'Mother Jones' or even 'the Widow Jones'.

It had been a difficult few years for Ann. She and Owen had operated a 'roadside refreshment room' that went broke in 1874.

Owen then worked on the railways, first at nearby Wangaratta and later at Bunyip in far-away Gippsland. In 1876, Ann bought her block of land near the railway line in Glenrowan and built a home. Two years later, her hotel was open for business. But tragedy struck in the spring of 1879 when Ann's second-oldest daughter, Ann Julietta, was killed in a tree-felling accident. It had been a terrible blow, but Ann still had five children to care for and by the winter of 1880 she was recovering.

Despite the absence of a husband—or perhaps because of it—Ann was starting to make something of herself. It may have presented a rough and unimposing appearance to the street but, as the archaeology would later prove, the Glenrowan Inn was very different inside. The five rooms were elegantly fitted out and the two fireplaces kept the place cosy and welcoming. The tables were covered with lace cloths and there were pretty knickknacks on the shelves. There was a clock on a mantelpiece and in the parlour there was a comfortable sofa for guests to relax next to the fire. One of the bedrooms was a little finer than the other, presumably for the better class of guest. The bar room was small but homely. Much of it was taken up by the counter where thirsty customers could drink their fill of wine, rum or brandy.

The thin redgum or stringybark boards of the walls were whitewashed on the outside and sealed on the inside with newspaper and hessian. Sheets of highly flammable calico insulated the ceiling. The floors were made of milled pine boards, without tongue or groove. The boards would have been laid green and, as they dried, gaps would have opened where small items could fall—a child's marble from Germany, say, or a sixpence, the price of a glass of beer. The owners of these items would never see them again but they would not be lost to history. The floorboards were covered with warm rugs and light from the kerosene lanterns glinted from glassware and pewter upon the furniture. The furniture was of good quality, on hire from a man in Wangaratta. Ann could not afford to buy the furniture, not yet anyway, but she was determined to make her country pub one of the finest in the district.

It was already a place she could be proud of. The sign she had erected at the front said it all:

The Glenrowan Inn
Ann Jones
Best Accommodation

A determined woman with a tendency to 'talk herself up', Ann was socially ambitious and outgoing. As a landlady, she had a respectable position in the community and she tried to blend into the shifting power bases of the unsettled Kelly Country by currying favour with both sides. She was crafty and careful. Above all, she was a single mother who wanted to protect her children even if it meant allying herself with the wrong people. She was serious about her business but she was playful and flirtatious when her life collided with Ned Kelly's that winter. Whether it was a case of self-preservation or something more basic, there is evidence of Ann getting quite personal with Australia's most infamous bushranger, a much younger man. And a fellow hostage felt Ann's daughter deserved 'six months in gaol' for getting a little too friendly with gang member Steve Hart.

Ann, who described her age as 'rising forty', was starting to break free of the poverty and hardship of her old life. She had been born a Kennedy in Tipperary, Ireland (also the home

Steve Hart, circa 1878. Photographer WE Barnes.
Image courtesy of the Pictures Collection, State Library of Victoria.

county of Ned Kelly's father, Red), and might have been a cousin to Sergeant Michael Kennedy who was killed by Ned at Stringybark Creek. Ann had endured the potato famine as a child before sailing to Australia in 1854, around the time of Ned's birth. She was fond of saying that her father, Lancelot, was the first white man to live in the nearby Buckland district, which was probably true, and that Lancelot was highly regarded by 'big men' in Ireland, which probably was not.

She married Owen Jones the year she arrived and the couple moved around the goldfields for some time before setting up their tearooms in Wangaratta. When the business went bankrupt, Owen left to find work. Ann did not seem to miss him much; her new inn was soon earning a profit of £30 a month and she was attracting a reasonable class of clientele.

Ann wanted to control her own destiny. In 'Ned's Women', an essay published in *Meanjin,* the La Trobe University historians Alex McDermott and Clare Wright examined the lives of the females of the Kelly story. In Ann Jones they found a woman determined to succeed:

> In the 19th century to be a licensed female publican was to be a woman of substance. Hotels were the hub of the community, and their proprietors could attain a superior social status unrivalled by any other female occupation. Hotel keeping was a tried and true route to social mobility, and Ann Jones was doing what she could to be on the fast track to success.

Popular history often sees the women almost as extras in the Kelly saga but their role was pivotal. Ned would never have taken up arms had his mother not been imprisoned for the attack on Fitzpatrick, and when he did, his sisters were there to support him. Ned liked women and he treated them with courtesy and respect. Much has been made of whether he had a love interest and there have always been curious claims—possibly first made by Ned himself—that he might secretly have married. Fans of the story have been looking for his true love ever since. He charmed and intrigued women and, in the fashion of the time, he behaved as a gentleman. Even Ann was not immune to his charms. It was a strange attraction that helped to define the course of the siege.

Despite her illness on the morning of the twenty-sixth, Ann had reason for optimism. She had been devastated by the death of Ann Julietta but her eldest son Thomas was working away from home and starting to do well. Thomas had helped Ann to build the inn and was sending money to her. As the owner of one of only two pubs in town, Ann had reason to expect that life would continue to get better. Glenrowan was not a wealthy town but agriculture was expanding and, more importantly, the railway promised to deliver a steady flow of visitors and income. Ann hoped this iron highway would bring wealth to her growing business.

In 1911, a newspaper reporter named Brian Cookson published an outstanding investigation into the Kelly story. Cookson worked for *The Sun* in Sydney but had lived in Melbourne as a boy. His links to Ned Kelly began when he was just a lad of nine. On 11 November 1880—the day of Ned's execution—the young Brian lunched at the table of Victoria's chief medical officer, Dr Edward Barker, who had that very morning seen Ned swing from the rope. Nine-year-old Brian must have been agog with excitement as he listened to tales of Ned's demise, and perhaps it was this moment that inspired him to make his journalistic visit to Kelly Country thirty years later.

Cookson wove a remarkable narrative of the people affected by the siege and its consequences. He painted poignant word pictures of a landscape drenched in winter rain, of chilly rural squalor in wooden huts, of a child's delights in simple pleasures and the stoic bravery of the survivors, three decades after the violence.

And Cookson told of a bedroom in a neat, painted cottage where 'there was nothing of brightness'. Here he met an old woman, sick and weary and full of woe. Ann Jones in her final days had much to tell about the events of June 1880.

Bitter and beaten, she had nothing good to say of the police, nor of the Kellys. Undoubtedly her version was skewed to suit herself but Cookson brings forth from Ann the anguish of a mother who has buried her children. Her grief for frail Johnny and doomed Jane is palpable and Cookson seemed to feel sorrow for Ann as she waited to die alone in her little wooden cottage.

Her conversation with the reporter also illustrated the impossible position that fate had dealt her. In one of a series of articles in *The Sun*, Ann told Cookson of being trapped between the police and the Kellys, and of the price it cost her family.

> They [the police] blamed me for most of the things the Kellys did . . . I had nothing whatever to do with them. And that is the truth. They accused me of hiding them. The place only had five rooms, and there was no hiding place in it. I didn't hide anyone . . . But that awful night! The place full of people and the Kelly crowd with pistols and guns! And my poor, innocent children! Think of that . . . Six of them, helpless, in that crowded place and the bullets flying through it.

Ann remembered the slight and frail Johnny as 'such a quiet and clever boy'. She recalled quiet, clever Johnny lying in agony on the hotel floor, screaming for his mother and bleeding from a fatal bullet wound. Ann was overcome with grief as she told Cookson of the desperate fight to save her son, 'his poor little white face . . . turned up, the eyes looking into mine as though imploring help'. She told the reporter that Jane, too, 'a dear, brave little woman', was hit by a bullet, and she told of the fire that left nothing standing of her home and business but the chimneys.

Talk at the bar that Saturday 26 June may well have turned to the Kelly outbreak. The gang had vanished after the raid on Jerilderie in February the previous year and the months since had been a time of rumour and uncertainty, marked by a futile police pursuit. The Kellys were the talk of the newspapers and Ann was well aware that she was living in dangerous times. The gang's supporters usually drank at McDonnell's, but it is likely they began visiting the Jones' hotel in the months before the siege. For Ann, the intense police activity in the north-east was good for business. Her refusal to choose a side, however, was risky and it was hard to know who to trust. At the centre of the intrigue was an outlaw gang with £2000 on each head, dead or alive. An informer could make a fortune, or lose a life.

For twenty months, Ned and his men had evaded capture. They hid with sympathisers, in caves or in the bush, always nearby but never close enough to grab. Francis Hare later noted that the outlaws had geography on their side. Their family homes at Greta, in the Woolshed Valley and Wangaratta were divided by three rugged ranges. It meant the gang could hide in the hills close to their homes and when word reached them that the police were approaching, the Kellys could simply melt away into the next range.

In his book, *The Last of the Bushrangers*, Hare wrote:

If, for instance the police made up their minds to search the interminable ranges at the back of Greta, extending for over one hundred miles, the outlaws would, through their sisters, get the information furnished to them that the police were in that district and they would shift their position during the night to the Warby Ranges, at the back of Hart's place; if parties of police were sent there, they would move over to Byrne's friends. In this manner they could find retreats over hundreds of miles of impenetrable mountains, amongst which they had been brought up all their lives, and where they knew every road, gully and hiding place.

There were late night food drops and stolen times with loved ones at isolated farms and glens across Kelly Country. An army of sympathisers closed ranks around the gang, protecting them and urging them on. Beechworth's *The Ovens and Murray Advertiser* estimated there were at least 800 supporters, 'not at all tempted by the reward offered for their apprehension'. The paper did not say how it arrived at this number; there may have been more.

The gang had committed only two robberies but the authorities were enraged by their failure to capture them. They had broken out to stage the Euroa and Jerilderie robberies and then, just as quickly, they had melted back into the bush. They were seen everywhere and found nowhere. They were an embarrassment to the colonial police and government. Victoria was becoming a laughing stock and questions were even being asked in London.

The pressure grew each day the Kellys remained free—but the net was closing. The new telegraph technology was now pitted against the traditional bush variety and the arrival of steam rail meant police on trains could outpace men on horseback. The supporters were numerous but there were many others who bore no love for the gang. Some were neutral, others were frightened into silence and some were actively hostile. Informers were an ever-present threat.

Capture or death was inevitable. The gang could have fled overseas, perhaps to America, but for Ned it had gone far beyond a simple case of cops and robbers. Desperate and soon to be cornered, Ned and his men would strike back. But the police were everywhere, many corrupt and unscrupulous, and under enormous pressure. Nobody could be sure who was being watched or who might be an informer and rumours spread like a bushfire in February. Drinkers at Ann's bar on the afternoon of 26 June might have heard the gossip and added their own. Those in the know would have been wise to keep their own counsel. As the murder of Aaron Sherritt would show, loose lips could be permanently silenced.

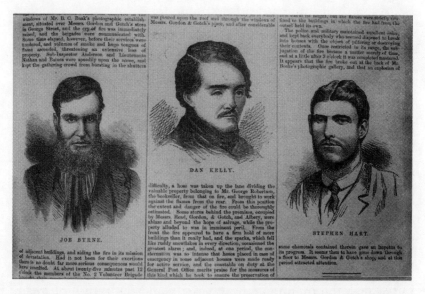

Extract from a newspaper with portraits of Joe Byrne, Dan Kelly and Stephen Hart. Image courtesy of the Pictures Collection, State Library of Victoria.

Judith Douthie, a grandmother with a deep interest in Ann Jones' story, spent years learning about Ann and the others who were taken hostage at Glenrowan. She had a particularly personal interest in two of the hostages—Thomas Curnow and David Mortimer—because she is related to both. Curnow was her great-great-uncle and Mortimer was her great-grandfather on her father's side. Her research culminated in the publication of a book, *I Was at the Kelly Gang Roundup*, which recounts the stories of all the hostages known to have been held at the inn.

At least sixty-two people were under the gang's control when the Kellys took over Glenrowan and more than forty were still in the pub when the bullets began to fly. Some of them wanted to be there. Most were forced at gunpoint. A handful would not survive and some of those who did would carry scars for life. And of all them, Ann Jones was one of the least remembered but most important. Judith Douthie sees Ann as a wily woman with a 'chip the size of a woodpile on her shoulder'. She hoped the dig would bring her closer to under-standing Ann and explain why she took the course she did.

Judith also hoped to rehabilitate the reputation of her great-great-uncle, the Glenrowan schoolmaster, Thomas Curnow. In a story that demands its characters be hero or villain, his-tory tagged Thomas as the latter. He saved dozens—perhaps hundreds—of lives and paid for it by spending the rest of his life looking over his shoulder. Judith believes Thomas has been misjudged and that he deserves a better epitaph in the history books. But her most poignant image of the siege belongs to David Mortimer, who was there when Ann Jones' son was hit by a police bullet. 'All his life my great-grandfather said he could never forget the horrifying screams as little Johnny Jones lay dying on the floor,' she said.

Whatever happened at the Glenrowan Inn on the night of the twenty-sixth, it is known for certain that Ann was asleep in bed after midnight. For it was there that Ned Kelly roused her from sleep and made her one of the first prisoners in the Glenrowan affair. Other hostages soon followed. Within twenty-four hours almost everybody in town was rounded up and Ann found herself at the centre of a rollicking party to which most of the guests were invited at gunpoint.

Among them were Martin Cherry, a 'jolly Irishman' whose curiosity cost him his life, and James Reardon, a railway worker who secretly tried to avert a disaster only to see his family threatened with death at the hands of a policeman. There was the carter John Lowe, who lived to tell of the siege's aftermath, and his boss, Alfonso Piazzi, an Italian quarryman who was most displeased to be dragged from the bed he was sharing with a lady friend. Labourer George Metcalf was there, too. He was shot in the eyes and died within months. The last man taken hostage, the policeman Hugh Bracken, bravely escaped the siege and then saved Ned Kelly's life—so Ned could face the gallows. And, in turn, that brave act contributed to the policeman's early death.

A farmer named Robert Gibbons told of women screaming as 'bullets rattled around the house' and the teenaged Tom Cameron wrote a powerful letter describing the drama as it unfolded. The stationmaster, John Stanistreet, and his wife Emily were taken prisoner at gunpoint and a young man named John Delaney was left shaking in fear at a threat of murder.

Others were there as part of the plan—Kelly supporters could largely come and go as they wished—but in the end more than forty souls were imprisoned in a wooden box when the shooting began. Farmers and railwaymen, merchants and labourers, they would witness a blood-soaked battle that would instantly become legendary. And they would be there when Ann Jones made a fatal mistake.

6
IN SEARCH OF THE INN

'If we don't find it . . .'

By the end of the fourth day at the dig, the top layers of grass and soil had given up all sorts of odds and ends. There were hundreds, perhaps thousands, of items either on the ground or just under the surface. Appropriately for a battle site, there were shells from rifles and shotguns but these were modern discards—evidence of recent hunting. There were also one-cent and two-cent coins, broken plates, spark plugs, bent spoons and cheap jewellery—some of which was probably left by the last people to live there more than thirty years earlier. The decades before and since that time had left a swathe of refuse—bottle tops, flattened cans, chunks of brick, broken tiles—detritus of the throwaway twentieth century—and most of it had to be collected and assessed before it could be thrown away one final time.

The team had now cleared a large square of earth from the front quarter of the block. This space was thought to cover the whole of Ann's inn, from the verandah posts at the front to the guest bedrooms at the back and beyond. A smaller, shallower square of topsoil had been carved off a section directly behind the inn. Based on the photographic evidence, this square would be directly over Ann Jones' kitchen and residence. This secondary square was a token start on the team's plans to excavate the residence but it had gone no further. At least for now the focus remained on finding the inn.

The excavation of the inn had reached a depth of three or four centimetres, enough to expose the first signs of the final occupation layer. Lines of intriguing brickwork had been revealed and small items such as old nails and melted balls of glass had been found in layers of demolition rubble. It was too early to say for sure, but it seemed likely that agriculture or building activity had scrambled up these relics from the bottom occupation levels into the topsoil. Coins and a medallion from the early twentieth century had also turned up and there were hopes of finding some even older, maybe even dated right back to the original inn.

The next day there were cheers at an apparent breakthrough. A brass cartridge from a police Martini-Henry rifle had turned up in a small test trench in what was thought to be the breezeway behind the inn. The trench was quickly widened to reveal three more cartridges left in a scatter pattern by the men who had fired them. It was clear proof of police activity in colonial times and Adam Ford was delighted. Because of their location at the rear of the inn, it had him wondering whether it was evidence of the police attacking the back of the pub. There was also speculation that these were the shells used by the police to shoot the Kellys' horses on the final day of the siege. As it turned out, however, the cartridges were later identified as a rolled brass type not widely in police use until later in the 1880s. Exciting as they were, the shells had been fired and discarded after the siege ended.

A discovery lifts the team's hopes. Courtesy Reece Rayner and Neal Kelly.

But that disappointing news was still to come. By now, the dig had also turned up more lead splats, so along with the rifle shells there were some solid exhibits to show. National and local media were scheduled to visit soon and Ford was glad to have something to show them.

The early discoveries also helped to satisfy one of the dig's main aims—the preservation and recording of any finds that may not have survived indefinitely. There was always a risk that further looting or organic degradation such as rusting could eventually destroy or displace some of the archaeology but the recovery of the bullets and shells meant that a small part of the site's history had been preserved and that one of the dig's targets would be met. On the other hand, progress had been even slower than expected. It was always going to be a complicated job with a century of occupation to sift through, but the sheer amount of the material to be removed, recorded and discarded was threatening to put the dig behind schedule.

Encouragingly, though, an excavator was now on site and when Ford was sure any archaeology in the top layers had been preserved, he called in the machine to do the grunt work. In no time at all, the excavator uncovered the rest of the brickwork that had been poking through the top of the trench. When the archaeologists moved back in with picks, shovels and trowels, they revealed a perfect floor plan of a solid brick building with several rooms. As more soil was scraped away, neat brick drains were found leading towards Siege Street. These works were the foundations and water drains of the wine shanty, now opened to fresh air for the first time in thirty-two years. The size and shape of the brickwork gave a clear indication of just how substantial the shanty had been and a better understanding of how it might have affected the inn.

The zigzagging brick foundations were not the target of the dig but they could not be ignored. They had to be cleared, mapped and recorded before the team could move on to the next stage. As new walls were discovered, they were painstakingly exposed by spade and trowel. Ford described the following of the walls as a 'secret guilty pleasure for archaeologists', giving as they did a sense of tangible discovery to the site's history. It was time-consuming but it added to the understanding of the site.

There was also a little false thrill for those hoping to find a mythical cellar. In the south-western corner—where Siege Street met Beaconsfield Parade—the excavator had uncovered a square, brick-lined shaft that descended to a dirt-filled bottom. Alas, this cellar belonged to the shanty, not the inn. It was no surprise to find it there as the property owner Linton Briggs clearly remembered it being filled in when the shanty was demolished thirty-two years earlier but the team needed to know how much damage the cellar had caused and whether the backfill contained anything of worth. It was thought the cellar had cut right through a section of Ann's parlour and verandah. If so, that part of the inn would be lost. Archaeologist Caroline

Wilby was given the job of finding out by removing the backfill by hand. It was a long, laborious and eventually almost fruitless task. The rubble fell lower, slowly exposing the smooth brick walls of the cellar, which appeared to contain . . . nothing.

Eventually, though, the cellar gave up its only contents: two halves of a white ceramic bottle that were wedged into the bottom corner. A stamp on the glazed stoneware revealed it to be a bottle of 'Ye Old English Style Brewed Ginger Beer' made by a now-defunct brewery in nearby Wangaratta in the early 1900s. A nice reminder of a simpler time before plastics, it had lain broken and forgotten on the floor of the cellar for years. Like the shanty itself, however, it was a distraction from the real target.

Archaeologist and former soldier Jon Sterenberg drove a tank in Germany in the 1970s and later went into a particularly grim field of forensic archaeology. As part of war crimes investigations he had excavated mass graves from the Balkan civil war. He had also helped British police by exhuming gangland murder victims. When it came to digging, he had pretty much seen it all but was quick to lighten the mood with a dry but infectious sense of humour. Like Ford, Sterenberg was from the Birmingham region in northern England. He enjoyed saying 'fair dinkum' and 'beauty, mate' in a distinctive Brummy accent. While he was digging at the front of the Glenrowan site, just under Ann's verandah, he let out a triumphant whoop to a film crew covering the dig. He had found a revolver. Indeed he had—a child's cap gun from the 1970s. It brought chuckles and a moment of nostalgia for those old enough to remember such toys but it brought the team no closer to the inn.

Progress slowed further in the second week, thanks to a series of minor setbacks, mainly weather-related. Heavy showers occasionally swept across town, sending the diggers ducking for cover and muddying the bottom of the trenches. Also, the grass at the back of the field was infested with three-cornered 'cat-head' prickles that shredded the wheelbarrow tyres, delaying the soil sifting, and work was halted for a short time when a visiting workplace safety official required the installation of extra fencing and signage. On top of all that, the information coming out of the dig was becoming increasingly hard to interpret and Ford was frustrated at the difficulty in pinpointing the remains of the hotel.

It was not that nothing had been found. On the contrary, the earth between the shanty foundations had been pared back to reveal all sorts of archaeological evidence. There were plenty of post holes, proof of burning in tiny chunks of charcoal, and even molten glass with rounded edges that indicated a fire of extreme temperatures. Two buildings had been burnt down on the site; now there was evidence of at least one of those fires. These were useful indicators that success was close but much of the data was proving to be confusing.

There was almost too much information for the team to identify the inn's remains. Ford's earlier statement that 'you can't hide a hole in the ground' had proved uncomfortably accurate. The problem was not a lack of post holes but rather an excess of them. They appeared everywhere—circular discolourations in the ground, some still retaining splintered lengths of hardwood. Each one told a tale of the site's history but so far they were tales without an ending.

Over the rest of the week more post holes became evident as the soil between the shanty foundations was scraped away. It should have been good news; upright posts were the essential foundations of Ann's hotel and their remains should have provided a floor plan for the inn. But other buildings had been constructed on the site, not long afterward, by the same method of erecting timber posts as foundations. It was like trying to find a pattern of footprints on a crowded beach. Which holes belonged to the inn and which came later?

And, through a quirk of electronic fate, data that had been mapped and collected with a machine called a 'total station' had vanished. This machine, which looked much like a surveyor's theodolite, created a three-dimensional record of the site. The data was essential for recording purposes and it would cost the team two days to re-gather the lost information. And they still had not found the inn. By the end of the eleventh day, Adam Ford was preparing for the worst. 'I'm a little cheesed off, frankly,' he said. 'I don't like to think it but there's always the possibility we won't find what we're looking for. If we don't find it [the inn] we'll have a big problem.'

It was a rare moment of pessimism for Ford. The dig that had promised so much now seemed to be delivering so little, and the thought nagged at him. It would take two stains in the dirt to revitalise his hopes. Those stains—black and pink—would provide some of the crucial information to pinpoint Ann Jones' elusive inn.

7
AT WAR WITH THE LAW

'We don't like Ned Kelly.'

By the second week, archaeologists, students and volunteers had transformed the narrow corner block. They had shifted a huge amount of soil from the front quarter of the site and it was now piled in big mounds along the edges. The students were busy sifting the soil for artefacts and putting the finds aside for assessment. There was a stream of tour buses and cars coming and going and the number of workers, tourists and official visitors had swelled to the point where parking was at a premium in Siege Street and Beaconsfield Parade. In fact, there were so many cars and trucks restricting access to homes that somebody called the police.

Two officers in reflector sunglasses arrived in a marked car and stood at the fence. Without entering the field, they instructed Adam Ford to have the offending cars removed. The police—both male—were professional but detached, and started to leave once their directive was carried out. They politely but firmly refused an offer to tour the site.

'No, thanks,' said one. 'We don't like Ned Kelly.'

Police, as a rule, do not like Ned Kelly at all and Victoria Police like him the least. Many are especially offended by the trend in recent years to glorify Ned, a man they see as a cop killer and bank robber. In 2010, the secretary of the Victoria Police Association, Senior Sergeant Greg Davies, spoke for many police when he said:

If people are going to lionise Ned Kelly, they need to realise that he was a murdering thief and armed robber and lout—and they might as well lionise [multiple-murdering gangster] Carl Williams.

Davies says Ned Kelly was no Robin Hood and that if he 'hadn't worn a tin hat nobody would know who he was today'.

Other police will say that Ned was a violent criminal who deserved what he got, just like other executed murderers in unmarked graves at old prisons around the country. It is not true of all police, but generally they do not like Ned Kelly one bit. You might think that after some 130 years they would get over it. After all, it was a long time ago and the police hardly covered themselves in glory during the Kelly outbreak. To understand their perspective, it helps to put oneself into a copper's boots. A bad day at work for many of us could involve, say, a paper cut or maybe a tongue lashing from the boss. On a bad day at work, a cop can be killed or maimed. Since 1853, about 150 Victorian police officers have been killed while on duty, many of them murdered. Despite the worst efforts of Melbourne's *Underbelly* gangsters in later times, Ned Kelly remains the biggest single killer of Victorian police officers. This is something that police have not forgotten.

Ned was in trouble with the law from an early age. In 1869, when he was aged about fourteen, the Kelly family received a visit from a colourful Irishman known as Harry Power. Harry made a living by robbing mail coaches and business was booming. He had escaped from gaol and now needed an apprentice to help with his work. He had heard about the young Ned and thought he was just the boy for the job. Ned signed up and together they committed a number of robberies until shots were fired at the pair while they scoped out a station and Ned became frightened. Harry worried that Ned would get him caught and they parted company for a short time. Ned did not stay clear of trouble, however. In October 1869 he was acquitted of assaulting a Chinese pig and fowl dealer named Ah Fook, and early in the next year he teamed up again with Harry Power. Ned was ready for the next stage of his training for a bushranging career.

Harry carried a double-barrelled shotgun that he used to threaten—but never shoot—his victims. He had gained a reputation as a gentleman robber and was always courteous to women. It seems likely that this rubbed off on Ned and helped him to set his own style as a chivalrous bandit. Among their last known raids was the robbery of Robert McBean, a pastoralist from Kilfera Station near Benalla. Harry and Ned relieved McBean of a watch with great sentimental value. The angry pastoralist was familiar with Ned and although the boy turned his face away during the robbery, McBean must have recognised him. For some reason, however, McBean told the police Harry was accompanied by a 'lad who rode on a brown horse' and Ned's identity was officially unknown. But Harry Power's identity was no secret and McBean chipped in £15 of his own money to add to the reward for Harry's capture. It might have been just enough to tip the balance against the old bushranger.

Harry had a mia mia—or bush lean-to—as a hide-out high in the steep cliffs overlooking the home of the Quinn clan in the upper reaches of the King Valley. Soon after the McBean robbery, Harry disappeared into his bush hideaway and lay low. He now had a £500 price on his head (plus McBean's £15) and, adding to his worries, Ned was arrested as his accomplice in May 1870. Ned was in custody for seven weeks, during which time he came under intense pressure to betray Harry. The boy did give away some useful information to the police but, it seems, not enough to lead them directly to the old bushranger. On 12 May, Ned stood trial at Benalla for the McBean robbery and was promptly acquitted for lack of evidence. He was not free yet, however. The police charged him with two other robberies committed with Harry Power and Ned remained in custody.

While Ned remained safely locked up, Assistant Commissioner Charles Nicolson and Superintendent Francis Hare set out with a search party to find Harry Power. It seems likely that they did indeed have a traitor to lead them to their quarry, but it was not Ned Kelly. It was almost certainly his uncle Jack Lloyd. Francis Hare later identified a mysterious informer known only as 'L—' as the man who reluctantly led the police in an early morning raid through the Quinn stronghold and up into the craggy bush where Harry was caught, asleep in his humpy. If the traitor was Jack Lloyd, he qualified for a £500 reward. It's likely that another uncle, Jimmy Quinn, was also involved in the betrayal and the money might have been shared, but Ned got none of it. He was, however, widely blamed as the traitor, especially by Harry Power, who had seven years in Pentridge to think about it. Harry went straight after his release and held a number of legitimate jobs until he drowned in 1891. He and Ned never met again and, quite wrongly, Harry forever remembered his protégé as a coward and traitor.

Two weeks after Harry's arrest, Ned was acquitted of the final robbery charge against him. He had been in custody for seven weeks, during which time he'd undergone intense questioning from Hare and Nicolson. Hare thought poorly of Ned but Nicolson had a higher opinion of the lad they called 'Power's Mate'. It was at this time that Ned met a policeman who treated him fairly and tried to set him on a steadier course. Sergeant James Babington of Kyneton was a fatherly type who showed kindness to Ned as he waited to learn his fate. When Ned was acquitted, Babington even paid for Ned to stay in a Kyneton hotel for ten nights until he could make his way home. Ned promised to repay the money—three pounds five shillings —but two months later Babington was still waiting. He had to apply to the police department for reimbursement.

Ned's return to Greta marked the start of a difficult time. He was suspected by the police as a trainee bushranger and reviled by some in his own community for betraying Harry Power. Six weeks after returning home, Ned wrote to Sergeant Babington. The letter was lost in government files until 1985 and only came to light in 2000. The scrawled note—the only letter known to have been written in Ned's own hand—was a plea for help and at the same time, the first articulation of his sense of persecution.

I was writing these lines hoping to find you
and Mistr Nickilson
in good health as I am myself
at present I have arrived safe
and I would like you see
what you and Mstr. Nickelson
could do for me I have done
all circumstances would
allow me which you now
try what you con do answer
letter as soon as posabel
direct your letter to Daniel
Kelly greta post office
that is my name no more at presa[nt]
Edward Kelly
every one looks on me like
A black snake send me
an answer as soon as posable

Far from the snarling enemy of the police that he would become, Ned was just a boy losing his way and pleading for help. If all the police he dealt with had been as decent as Babington then Ned's life might have taken a different course. Instead, he was heading for more trouble with the law and, in particular, violent confrontations with three officers who would play key roles in his future.

Later that year, Ned found himself before the courts again when he was convicted of assaulting a former convict guard turned travelling hawker, Jeremiah McCormick. Ned may have been as much the victim as the villain here; McCormick wrongly blamed Ned for an unfortunate misunderstanding involving some calves' testicles. Another hawker named Gould had been in dispute with McCormick and gave Ned the testicles to pass on to McCormick's wife. The package contained a nasty note, presumably questioning McCormick's inability to father children, and violence erupted between the teenaged Ned and the hawker. It resulted in Ned's first prison sentence—six months' hard labour in the Beechworth Gaol.

The old gaol still stands in the centre of town. It was decommissioned when a new prison was built early in the twenty-first century but the razor wire and guard towers remain. Adjacent to green parkland, the old gaol is enclosed by great pale granite walls. In the afternoons, sunlight paints the walls a mellow gold, and the old prison seems almost rustic and peaceful. It recently opened as a tourist attraction and Ned's cell, number 101, is a central part of the tour. Of course, anyone who ever spent time on the inside of the walls would feel less kindly about the place. It was a tough place when it was built in 1859 and had hardly improved when Ned arrived there in November 1870.

He was released in March the following year but was in serious trouble just a month later when he received a horse from another flash young man, Isaiah 'Wild' Wright. Wild neglected to mention to Ned that the horse had been stolen and Ned, who perhaps did not ask, was caught in possession of it. He was violently arrested in Greta by the short-tempered policeman Edward Hall. A huge man, Constable Hall had already been involved in several brawls with the Kelly clan and during the arrest in Greta he tried to shoot Ned three times but the pistol misfired. Ned 'threw Hall in the dust' and the policeman retaliated by severely beating Ned with the revolver. In May, at the age of just sixteen, Ned Kelly was sentenced to his second prison term, this time for a three-year stint.

In August, Alexander Gunn—the husband of Ned's older sister Annie—was gaoled for stock theft and while Alexander and Ned were in prison Annie became pregnant—possibly to the Greta policeman Ernest Flood. Annie's baby arrived in November 1872 but two days later Annie died and was buried next to the Eleven Mile Creek. The baby died thirteen months later. Helpless in prison, the death of his sister infuriated Ned and he held a particular hatred for Constable Flood.

But first he had a score to settle with Wild Wright, and after he was released from prison in 1874, Ned called Wild to account. In August they fought a brutal and bloody bare-knuckle grudge match at Beechworth's Imperial Hotel. The hotel was demolished in the 1960s and two houses now stand in its place but a plaque marks the spot next to the Silver Creek where the two powerful young men battered each other in front of a hooting crowd. A picture taken by a Melbourne photographer at the time shows the nineteen-year-old Ned in his boxing trunks, fists raised and one foot thrust aggressively forward. It is a very striking image that captures Ned's great physical power and presence. Ned and Wild were equally tall and well built but Ned emerged from the fight—which may have lasted several hours—as the winner. Wild later admitted Ned had given him a hiding and Ned became the unofficial heavyweight champion of the north-east. Wild Wright later became one of Ned's greatest and most loyal supporters, and was at Glenrowan when Ned took the town hostage six years later.

Ned worked at a saw mill and stayed out of trouble for more than two years. His widowed mother Ellen had remarried in

1874. Her new husband, George King, was a shadowy American who claimed to have worked on the Californian goldfields. Their first child had arrived three months before the wedding and their third just a few days before Ellen was arrested for attempted murder in 1878. Little Alice King would spend much of her infancy in gaol with her mother.

George disappeared from Greta in late 1877 or early 1878 and Ellen never saw him again. It is not known where he went but he might have been on the run from the police. There have been suggestions that he ill-treated Ellen and was driven out. There is even a far-fetched story that Ned killed him, but Ned was on good terms with his stepfather, who was only a few years older. They had something else in common. They were both quite good at stealing horses and for several years during his time with Ellen, the American had joined the 'family business'.

In September 1877, Ned was falsely befriended by the policeman Constable Alexander Fitzpatrick, who might have spiked Ned's drink at a Benalla hotel and then framed him for being drunk and disorderly. The next day Ned was cuffed and marched by four policemen, including Fitzpatrick and Thomas Lonigan, from the Benalla lockup to the courthouse. Along the way he broke free and was chased into a bootmaker's shop where a violent brawl erupted. During the bloody struggle, Lonigan twisted Ned's testicles in a savage 'squirrel grip'. It was then that Ned is said to have roared his famous death threat: 'If ever I shoot a man, Lonigan, you will be the first!'

Relationships with the police were at a dangerous low, but they were about to get even worse.

It was on the evening of 15 April 1878—a Monday—that the notorious Fitzpatrick Incident took place, sending Ned's war with the law on a dark and irreversible course. It cemented an eternal enmity between the police and the Kellys and it sent the gang into hiding. Ultimately, the actions of the drunken and lecherous Fitzpatrick would be seen as the catalyst that made a fight to the death inevitable.

The Kelly family lived in a timber and bark hut that Ned had built for his mother at Eleven Mile Creek, near Greta, earlier that year. The house has long been lost and all that stands there now is a single brick chimneystack. Until recently, there were two chimneys in the flat paddock, which is studded by gum trees and divided by the shallow and often dry creek bed. One of the chimneys has now collapsed. There are conflicting views about the chimneys. Members of the Griffiths family, who own the land, are adamant the chimneys are the remains of a later building, while most historians are certain the ruins are those of the Kelly homestead.

There are also conflicting opinions about whether Ned was present at the family home on the day that Alexander Fitzpatrick called. Ned always denied he was there. In the Jerilderie Letter, he said he was 400 miles away. Because of accounts later made by Kelly family and friends, it seems highly likely that Ned was very much part of the drama that unfolded that evening. If so, it shows he was not above telling a very convincing lie, especially if it was for the sake of his beloved family. Either way, the clash between Fitzpatrick and the Kellys proved a defining moment in the Kelly story and Ned's younger sister Kate was a key player.

There was something about Kate. Like her sister Maggie, fifteen-year-old Kate was a gifted horsewoman who had the rather shocking habit of riding astride, rather than sidesaddle.

She could ride like the wind and with Maggie she helped to support the gang with food and information during their months on the run. After Ned's death, Kate became something of a celebrity, even taking her story to the stage in a sensational but short-lived attempt at a career as an entertainer. When she was about seventeen, Detective Michael Ward saw fit to describe her thus: 'Five feet four inches high, slender build, dark complexion and hair—thin features, dark piercing eyes, very small chin, fairly good looking and a reserved manner.'

KATE KELLY.

Wood engraving of Kate Kelly, published in the Illustrated Australian News, *3 July 1880. Image courtesy of the Pictures Collection, State Library of Victoria.*

The Ovens and Murray Advertiser managed to overcome its anti-Kelly feelings with genuine praise:

She has been described as a tall, dark and sublimely beautiful Lucretia Borgia kind of female [but the truth is] . . . She dresses invariably in black, and with taste; her voice is pleasing and soft; her manners gentle and quiet.

Kate had no shortage of admirers and as she entered her late teens there were plenty of potential suitors. To his detriment, Constable Alexander Fitzpatrick was among them. It has been said that Kate thought a relationship with him would be impossible. The twenty-two-year-old Fitzpatrick already had something of a record as a ladies' man. He had previously had a child by a young woman named Jessie McKay (they were not married but Fitzpatrick was providing her with financial support) and he was now engaged to a solicitor's daughter, Ann Savage, who was expecting his second child.

On the evening of the Fitzpatrick Incident, the constable arrived at the Kelly home fortified with a few stiff drinks from a hotel at Winton. He was there to arrest Dan Kelly for stock theft and, according to the Kelly version of events, Dan agreed to go with him, after he had eaten his supper. But violence broke out when something unsavoury transpired between Fitzpatrick and Kate Kelly. An approach was made: at the very least the policeman roughly pulled Kate onto his lap and asked for a kiss. Pandemonium erupted in the house. Then, with her family apparently under threat, Ellen Kelly belted the wayward constable over the head with a fire shovel, putting a dent in his helmet.

The policeman claimed Ned Kelly then appeared at the door and fired a shot that hit Fitzpatrick in the wrist. Fitzpatrick said he removed the ball with a knife and, conveniently, Ned was said to have kept the ball. This led to suggestions that the policeman inflicted the wound on himself. The policeman fled back to the hotel at Winton, where he steeled his nerves with a few more brandies and later filed a self-serving report about the events that had taken place in the Kelly home. As a result, Ellen Kelly was tried and—perhaps expecting to be gaoled for a few weeks on an assault charge—was instead sent to the Melbourne Gaol for three years for the attempted murder of a police officer.

The judge who sentenced her was Redmond Barry, the man who would send Ned to the gallows two years later. Ned's brother-in-law William Skillian (husband of Maggie) and his friend Bricky Williamson were also allegedly involved in the brawl and were gaoled for six years each. Skillian was particularly unlucky as it seems he was not at the Kelly house that evening and was wrongly identified by Fitzpatrick. The man identified as poor Skillian might in fact have been Joe Byrne.

Ned and Dan fled with attempted murder charges on their heads. Soon, they were outlawed and their feet set on the path to Glenrowan. Dan might never have seen his mother again and Ned would see her just a few more times as he waited for his date with the hangman.

In an article headed 'Murderous attack on a Constable', *The North Eastern Ensign* reported on 19 April that Fitzpatrick had been shot trying to arrest the 'young ruffian' Daniel Kelly. 'Nothing could be seen of the two Kellys,' reported the *Ensign*, 'but it is generally supposed they are hiding amongst the caves and fastness of the mountains . . .' The newspaper reported Ned as boasting that the police could not hunt him down as he was too well acquainted with the country and that 'he would never again be taken alive'. He was right on the first point and wrong on the second.

During Ellen's trial, the *Advertiser* dutifully reported the defence counsel's argument that Fitzpatrick's evidence was 'to a great extent a fabrication' but the newspaper also chose to agree with the sentence and to accept Fitzpatrick's version of events, albeit with reservations.

> ... no doubt he did colour the part of it relating to the wound inflicted a little—an error which young men of stronger brain power and better position have fallen into ere this.

It is hard to find anyone with a good word for Fitzpatrick. A superior officer later wrote that he 'associated with the lowest persons, could not be trusted out of sight and he never did his duty'. After Fitzpatrick was sacked from the police in 1880, Commissioner Standish said the ex-constable was 'generally bad and discreditable to the police force'. Fitzpatrick ended up moving to Melbourne, where he listed his occupation as 'traveller'. And Ned Kelly, although hardly an impartial observer, said in the Jerilderie Letter that Fitzpatrick was never 'known to be one night sober and that he sold his sister to a Chinaman'. More than a century later, ninety-four-year-old Elsie Pettifer, who was Ned's niece and the granddaughter of Ellen Kelly, put it just as bluntly when she told *The Age* in 1998: '[Fitzpatrick] was a mongrel. He came out there drunk. He came out there and he tried to maul Kitty. Granny hit him over the head with a shovel.'

Fitzpatrick lied about much that took place on that Monday evening but he may well have been telling the truth when he said that Ned was present. Regardless, Fitzpatrick goes down as one of the villains in the piece. If not for him, the killings at Stringybark Creek would never have happened.

After the Fitzpatrick Incident, the Kellys fled into the wilderness of forest and mountain in the Wombat Ranges near Mansfield. The police were soon hunting for Ned and Dan—along with two persons unknown. Those two could have been any of the Kellys' mates but it was Joe Byrne and Steve Hart who would become wanted men. Remarkably, Steve is believed to have made the decision to join the gang on the spur of the moment. Toiling on a tedious job on the family farm near Wangaratta, Steve is said to have thrown down his tools, crying: 'Here's to a short life but a merry one!' He galloped off to join Ned and Dan. Soon they would be known as the Kelly Gang.

They felt reasonably safe in the alpine forest, where they set up a whiskey still, using a heavily fortified cabin as a base. They also had some luck sluicing for gold in the mountain creeks. Although lightly armed, they spent hours perfecting their aim by firing at targets on a tree. Tom Lloyd, Aaron Sherritt and possibly other members of the Greta Mob kept them company and, with a network of supporters, they were able to hide in safety. But the police had no intention of allowing the Kellys to roam free and, in October of that year, two heavily armed mounted parties were sent into the forest to find them.

The police arrived from the north and south in a pincer movement. As well as provisions and weapons, their horses carried leather straps that could be used to ferry out corpses. The police were all in plain clothes (as was normal practice) and they carried more ammunition than prescribed by the authorities. Heavily armed and boasting of their readiness to kill the fugitives, they had added to their weaponry by borrowing a shotgun from the vicar of Mansfield. Were the slings and extra ammunition evidence that they intended to kill the Kellys?

Or were they reasonable precautions for men preparing for an armed confrontation? Kelly supporters later used the leather belts to validate Ned's claim of self-defence, saying they prove the police set out from the beginning to bring the Kellys out of the forest dead. For their part, police have always maintained the officers were there to fulfil their lawful obligation to arrest the fugitives. In any case, the slings were never used.

The pursuers made no secret of their arrival, lighting fires at night and shooting at birds and animals. The Kellys—forewarned by supporters that the police were in the forest—had no problem finding and surrounding one police party as they set up camp near the banks of the now infamous Stringybark Creek. Two police, Thomas McIntyre and Thomas Lonigan, were minding the camp and the other two, Michael Kennedy and Michael Scanlan, were scouting the bush for the gang. Crouched in the thick scrub around the clearing, the Kellys could easily have gunned down the two unsuspecting police at their campsite. Instead, Ned shouted, 'Bail up!' and one of the officers, McIntyre, surrendered. The other—Lonigan—did not.

What happened in the confused and bloody moments that followed has been debated ever since. Three days after the shooting, McIntyre told Superintendent John Sadleir that Lonigan was ducking for cover and reaching for his pistol to fire at the gang when Ned shot him in the eye. This is the version that Ned always maintained was the truth. But later, McIntyre changed his story and said—on oath—that Ned killed Lonigan in cold blood. Either way, Lonigan—the man Ned Kelly had once threatened to kill—was dead and McIntyre was held hostage.

When Kennedy and Scanlan returned to the campsite, Ned again called out 'Bail up!' Mayhem erupted, men and horses panicked, shots rang out from both sides and Kennedy and Scanlan were hit. Scanlan was killed. It is possible that Joe Byrne fired that fatal shot but Ned always took the blame for it. Kennedy fired a total of eleven shots as he retreated through the thick forest and Dan Kelly was lightly wounded in the shoulder. Ned pursued the mortally wounded Kennedy through the bush, where the policeman crashed to the ground. He had lost his gun and Ned could see Kennedy would not survive. In one of the many contrasting facets to the Kelly story, Ned comforted the policeman as he lay slowly dying in the bush. They spoke of the officer's wife and five surviving children and then Ned put the shotgun the police had borrowed in Mansfield to the stricken Kennedy's chest and pulled the trigger. Was it a mercy killing, or murder? We've been debating it for more than a century.

Ned and his men robbed all three police of weapons, money and rings before respectfully covering Kennedy's body. Joe Byrne was wearing Scanlan's ring on the day of his death at the bar of Ann Jones' inn. It was claimed, rather extravagantly, that the gang severed one of Sergeant Kennedy's ears as a trophy. Ned vehemently denied it, and it is far more likely that animals or birds disfigured the policeman's body. But the gang did rob Kennedy of a gold watch. Later, the stolen watch would become central in the healing of the rift between the police and the Kelly supporters.

As the shots rang out, the unarmed Thomas McIntyre fled on Kennedy's horse. He claimed to have been fired at as he galloped away but it is possible he was only hearing the sounds of the gunfight with Scanlan and Kennedy. Fearing pursuit, McIntyre sheltered that night in a wombat hole, where he wrote notes about the gunfight. He was accused of cowardice by some in the press but lived to give evidence against Ned in his murder trial.

The dying Sergeant Kennedy might have asked Ned to deliver a letter to his wife. Ned later denied this but pages from Kennedy's notebook were found at the scene so it may well have been true. If there was a letter, the policeman's widow never received it and neither she nor their children learned of Kennedy's final thoughts. One of the children was a boy called James, who grew up to have his own family. James's grandson, also named Michael Kennedy, is now a serving police officer at Stanhope in northern Victoria. Senior Constable Mick Kennedy joined the force in 1971 and in the early days he did not have particularly strong feelings against the Kellys, despite the killing of his great-grandfather. But like many other police, he eventually grew to resent the growing celebration of Ned Kelly as a 'postcard hero'.

Mick Kennedy does not believe the police were sent to the forest to kill the Kellys. He is convinced they were doing then what they still do now—legally carrying out an arrest warrant for wanted criminals. And with a policeman's crime-scene logic, he believes there is no doubt that the killing of his great-grandfather was a deliberate murder: 'He [Sergeant Kennedy] was retreating backwards for 200 metres through thick scrub so how they can say it [Ned's shooting of Kennedy] was self-defence is beyond me.'

But Ned Kelly always claimed the police killings were in self-defence. He also frequently expressed regret that Kennedy died and said the sergeant was the 'bravest man he'd met'. It is cold comfort to his descendant and namesake. Mick Kennedy bears no grudges against anyone living today but believes Ned Kelly was the murderer of three policemen and should be remembered that way. Kennedy had five children. He was thirty-six when he died. Scanlan had no children and lived with his sister. He was thirty-five. Lonigan was a father of four. He died at the age of thirty-seven.

Today, a dirt road winds through the thick sub-alpine forest in the Wombat Ranges. The road continues high into the mountains, the very fastness that sheltered the Kelly Gang 130 years ago. Before it climbs into the wilderness, the road leads to a small grassy clearing in the soaring mountain gums and eponymous stringybarks. A stone monument stands in the clearing. It carries a plaque inscribed with three names: Sergeant Michael Kennedy, Constable Michael Scanlan and Constable Thomas Lonigan. The plaque reads:

Killed at Stringybark Creek on the 26th of October 1878 during the execution of their duty in a gunfight with a group of men later known as the Kelly Gang, respectfully remembered and never forgotten.
The Victoria Police Force

There can be a great silence in the bush. Sometimes all that can be heard is the call of birds—the inappropriate chuckle of a kookaburra, maybe, or the more fitting and mournful lament of a crow. At ground level, the daylight hours are quiet but a visitor might hear the soft scurry of a fleeing lizard or the rhythmic thump of a wallaby in the scrub. Ferns grow tall from damp gullies and bright moss clings like a winter coat to rocks and fallen logs. Even in this dry and wide brown land, the clearing often glistens with mountain showers dripping from a million leaves. The grey mist seems to float among the towering eucalypts, giving a sad dignity to this lonely monument in its quiet clearing.

The monument was erected in 2001 after a Benalla detective watched the opening ceremony of the 2000 Olympic Games in Sydney. Detective Leading Senior Constable Peter Clifford noted the ceremony included a tribute to artist Sidney Nolan's iconic Ned Kelly images and it was being beamed out to millions of people around the world. To Clifford, Australia was celebrating 'a murderer responsible for the deaths of three police'. Peter Clifford had trained with a young policeman, Damian Eyre, who was murdered with his colleague Steven Tynan in Melbourne's notorious Walsh Street murders in 1988 and Clifford found an uncomfortable parallel between the Walsh Street and Stringybark Creek killings. 'And I thought, in 100 years time are we going to hold up the persons responsible for the [Walsh Street] murders as heroes as well? Because they thought they were fighting for a cause, too,' he said in 2010.

Descendants of the Kellys and the murdered police attended the official opening in 2001, among them Senior Constable Mick Kennedy and Ned Kelly's great-great nephew Leigh Olver. It was a rewarding moment for both men. They got on well and agreed the actions of their ancestors were no cause for personal dispute today. Melbourne's *Herald Sun* published a photograph of them with the headline, 'Kelly bad blood washed away'. It had been more than 120 years but it helped to break down some of the final barriers.

8
CAUGHT IN A TRAP

'I had to tear up some rails or he would shoot me.'

At the time of the siege, a post-and-rail fence divided the railway reserve from the road opposite the inn. In 2008, Adam Ford dug a small trench in the area and found the post holes from the now-vanished fence. He also found a rusty stain, about twice the size of a matchbox. It had obviously been a metal container and because of its depth and the undisturbed nature of the area, Ford—with input from Ian Jones—was able to link it with a group of men who played a small but important role in the siege.

The rusty stain appeared to have been a tin that had probably contained sardines or something similar. If so, it might have been the remains of a meal eaten by road workers camped there on the night before the siege. Led by the Italian quarryman Alfonso Piazzi, the men were collecting gravel from a hill at Glenrowan to be used in roadworks at Benalla, about 24 kilometres to the south-west. They slept in white canvas tents. A cart stood next to the fence, ready for use the next morning.

But the gravel carters would not get to work that day because in the early hours of the morning of 27 June Ned Kelly and Steve Hart crept up to the roadside reserve demanding help at gunpoint.

Piazzi and his men had just settled down for another cold night outdoors. Their only protection from the freezing weather was the small canvas tents and whatever bunks and bedding that could be stored inside. Piazzi, however, had a little help. Snuggled inside his tent, he had a lady friend to keep him warm on that cold night.

Several of the hostages later told of a 'strange woman from Benalla' at Ann Jones' inn as the siege unfolded. That woman was undoubtedly Piazzi's friend but much about her remains a mystery. It was clearly a scandal and, understandably, neither she nor Piazzi were keen to discuss their relationship. The 'strange woman' lives on in the story, though, mainly due to the amusement she provided to Piazzi's workmates. They had been up late that night and, as the carter John Lowe recalled sixty years later, there was some 'jollification' at the boss's expense:

> . . . one of our mates had a female visitor from Benalla with him in his tent, and we were doing all we could to annoy him, and having some fun.

At midnight, with their fun over, the road workers had settled for the night, ready for another day's work on the gravel pit. What they could never have expected was to have been dragged from their beds by the most infamous men in the colony. The amorous Alfonso Piazzi and his navvies had not been part of Ned's plan to derail the train, but as the plan began to unravel the road gang would become the first people in Glenrowan to be drawn into the plot.

About three hours after the murder of Aaron Sherritt, Ned Kelly and Steve Hart had sneaked into Glenrowan under the cover of darkness. They brought with them a bomb and two more suits of armour. Late in the evening, about nine o'clock, they had secretly watched the last train pass through the town. By this time Aaron was dead and the other members of the gang, Dan and Joe, were on their way to Glenrowan, expecting a police train to be dispatched from Melbourne at any moment. Ned and Steve planned to pull up the rail on the high point just north of the town, where they expected the train to crash at high speed into the steep gully. They were also carrying a bomb—a drum of blasting powder. As a postscript to the destruction of the train, Ned intended to blow up the rail line south of Benalla. This would halt rail traffic into Benalla from either direction, allowing the gang and their supporters to plunder a bank there. These funds would be used to finance the uprising or maybe even the new republic of north-eastern Victoria.

Ned and Steve deposited the gunpowder and some packhorses at or near McDonnell's Hotel. Kelly sympathisers—including Ned's first cousin and great mate Tom Lloyd—were gathering nearby, ready to swoop once the train had crashed. The sympathisers had Chinese rockets ready to fire, to signal the start of the uprising.

But first the rail line had to be uprooted. The gang knew there would be no trains the next day—a Sunday—and the first train to pass through would be the police special from Melbourne. Ned and Steve tried to pull up the rail lines late in the evening but soon found they had neither the skills nor the tools to do the job. The plot had hit its second major hurdle. They needed help and it seemed to Ned that Piazzi and his six workers could provide it. Soon after midnight, Ned roused them from their beds. As well as a woman, the fiery Piazzi also had a gun in his tent and he did not take kindly to the intrusion. There was a struggle, a shot was fired into the ground and Piazzi's female friend let out a loud shriek. The gravel carter was quickly overpowered but Ned soon learned the men could not help. They were road workers, not railway men, Piazzi said, and could not do as Ned ordered.

Ned needed to rethink. It was then that Ann Jones became part of the slowly failing plot. Concerned that the gunshot and scream would raise the alarm, Ned marched the gravel carters over the road to the front of Ann's hotel, a distance of about 100 metres. As Steve guarded the men, Ned crept to the front of the inn and knocked loudly. 'Jump and answer the door!' he shouted. When there was no answer, he went to the building at the rear where Ann and her children lived. With another loud rap he roused fifteen-year-old Jane from her bed and Ann soon joined her. Ned now had Ann's entire family plus the seven road workers as hostages at the inn.

Ned had probably intended to use McDonnell's Hotel as the base for the uprising but now he chose Ann's instead. Perhaps he saw it as an opportunity to keep the sympathisers out of the action until they were needed. Maybe he also wanted to protect his publican (and republican) mate, Paddy McDonnell, but the ruckus at the campsite now meant Ann Jones was part of the equation. Ned did not trust Ann. He had every reason to think she was in league with the police. Those suspicions would be later borne out by Detective Michael Ward, who swore on oath that he had had frequent conversations with Ann at her pub and that she had promised to tell him if she could discover where the Kellys were. Ann had told Ward that Steve Hart's sister Ettie had been staying at the hotel and Ann would try to find out from her. Ned's sisters shared his distrust of Ann. Maggie and Kate knew Ann but 'would not speak to her'. They thought she was 'too much of a "traps" [police] woman'.

Ned still needed to pull up the rail lines or the uprising would fail before it started. He thought the solution lay in a cottage just across the road, to the south-west. This was the home of John Stanistreet, the stationmaster, and his wife Emily. They, too, were dragged from their beds at gunpoint. Stanistreet later said the door burst open and a man wearing an overcoat announced, 'I am Ned Kelly.' They must have been chilling words. Ned's name was instantly recognisable and his deeds the talk of the colony. While he'd shown himself to be a chivalrous bandit during the bank robberies at Euroa and Jerilderie, he was also a big man, heavily armed and living rough. Ned was not afraid to put the fear of God into those he opposed and John Stanistreet, as a respectable citizen and representative of the rail-ways, must have felt his family was in mortal danger. Like the others, he submitted at the point of Ned's revolver.

Some eighty years after the siege, historian Manning Clark painted a powerful word picture of Ned Kelly in *A History of Australia*, one that challenges the concept of Ned as a victim rather than a perpetrator. Clark wrote:

Ned Kelly was a wild ass of a man, snarling, roaring and frothing like a ferocious beast when the tamer entered the cage. Mad Ireland had fashioned a man who consumed his vast gifts in an insensate war on property and on all the props of bourgeois civilisation—the police, the bankers, the squatters, the teachers, the preachers, the railway and the electric telegraph.

If we can picture Ned in this way, then it is easy to understand why the civilians caught in his war meekly went along with his orders. The price of defying him would seem too high. Over the course of the next day and night, he would threaten some of his prisoners with death and casually discuss shooting others, including Ann Jones. Whether he meant them or not, some of the threats were taken very seriously and caused much fear. He harmed none of his hostages, however. In fact, several hostages later said Ned had treated them well. Some said they were more frightened of the police than of the outlaws.

But Ned now made it clear he would brook no opposition from Stanistreet. 'You have to come with me and take up the rails,' he said. Steve Hart backed up the demand by jabbing his rifle into the stationmaster's ribs, and adding: 'You get the tools out that are necessary to raise those rails.'

But like the gravel carters, John Stanistreet did not have the expertise to remove the rails and he had no option but to direct Ned towards men who did. These men were James Reardon and Dennis Sullivan, railway platelayers who lived further down the rail line. The Stanistreets and their six young children, meanwhile, became part of a growing group of townsfolk held hostage by the Kellys.

The Melbourne–Sydney rail line still follows much the same route as it did in 1880, except now there are two curving lines of shining steel tracks rather than the one that was there at the time of the siege. The tracks climb steadily to reach Glenrowan before beginning a descent past the town, where modern diesel locos pick up speed on the downhill stretch towards Wangaratta. As the tracks start to descend, they curve sharply to the left and pass over a deep, tangled gully. If you stand on the roadside reserve you can see the overgrown gully below, and imagine the impact of a train full of people and horses crashing over the uprooted tracks and down the steep embankment. The carnage would have been horrendous.

The debate about whether Ned was a hero or villain usually centres on the killing of the police at Stringybark Creek, and his penchant for robbing banks. It is possible to accept his successful stock thieving business as a last but defensible option for an oppressed colonial Irishman, and his admirers can balance his bank robberies with the view that he robbed from the rich to give to the poor. This is supported by the fact that after the gang's robberies, their impoverished friends and family suddenly had cash to pay their bills. And the gentlemanly manner in which Ned relieved the banks of their takings after bailing up entire towns makes it easier for some to forgive him for armed robbery. After all, he was only sticking up the rich symbols of the authorities.

The Stringybark Creek killings are more complex. Ned always claimed the police shootings were self-defence. 'This cannot be called wilful murder for I was compelled to shoot them, or lie down and let them shoot me,' he wrote in the Jerilderie Letter. And although he was eventually found guilty of murder for the shooting of Lonigan, Ned's supporters accept his claims that he was acting to save his own life. If his Glenrowan plot had come to fruition, however, we might now regard Ned in a very different way. He made no secret at the time of his intention to derail the train and admitted as much when police and reporters questioned him after he was captured. He said he had every intention of killing the people on the train because they would have killed him, if they could. This would have been a shocking act that would have had to be interpreted either as a declaration of war or an act of terrorism. And if the train had crashed, and if there had been an uprising, the empire would have dealt with the upheaval in its usual fashion—brutally and efficiently. Many people would have died and the victors would have written the history.

Historian Alex McDermott has raised hackles among some Ned fans for his work examining the darker side of the bushranger. McDermott sees Ned Kelly not as a romantic bandit but as someone who was part of a clan-based criminal network, and given to occasional outbursts of violence. McDermott completed his honours degree specialising in Kelly history and has edited and published a book on the Jerilderie Letter. He is held by some to be 'anti-Kelly' and to have taken a revisionist approach to the accepted history but McDermott prefers to see his work as the result of an independent investigation into a complex story. For him, holding up a light to the story of Ned Kelly revealed both Ned's remarkable strengths and fundamental flaws.

McDermott does not believe Ned was inherently bad; nor does he regard him as a hero. McDermott also notes that in the days before his execution, Ned changed his story, claiming he never intended to allow the train to crash and that he only pulled up the rails to frighten the authorities. But McDermott does not believe him.

> It's as clear as you can possibly get that he wanted to derail the train and probably kill all the survivors. Surely to God there are easier ways to force a train into stopping [than wrecking it].

Others can find convincing justification for Ned's plot. A descendant of the Lloyd and Hart families, Noeleen Lloyd, lives in the north-east and is a staunch defender of the Kellys and their friends. She believes the gang was not planning a crime so much as issuing a declaration of war. Noeleen Lloyd is quick to point out that the only people killed in the siege died at the hands of the police. Despite Ned's dire threats and the firing of hundreds of shots, the Kelly Gang killed nobody at Glenrowan. And, like many people, Lloyd believes Ned was the loser in a legitimate war with the authorities:

> He was committed, as were the boys, as were many, many members of the sympathisers to the fight for the republic of North East Victoria and they saw themselves as being at war. My belief is that they actually saw the deaths [on the police train] as necessary in a time of war. It was a fight not just for his family but for every family in the district and every family at large. It was about coming from England and Ireland and being treated in exactly the same way that they had been [in their homelands].

Historian Ian Jones has no doubt that Ned intended to derail the train but believes that he might have been reluctant to commit a massacre:

Ned simply wasn't ruthless enough to be a successful revolutionary. Ned wasn't a killer. All through his life he was remarkably reluctant to spill blood and I honestly think he was almost relieved when the plan began to become unstuck.

There is little doubt, however, that Ned hoped to spark an uprising and it is likely that he did indeed plan to create a local republic, or at the very least use a combination of force and politics to find a solution to his problem. There were few other options. His mother was still in prison, his family was being harassed and the police net was closing. As the last of the bushrangers, twenty-five-year-old Ned would have been aware the life expectancy of outlaws was short. Few made it into their thirties. Unless he fled Australian shores, perhaps to America, his only hope was to roll the dice. It would be a case of death or glory for the Kelly Gang.

Ian Jones believes the crashing of the train was meant to ignite the uprising that could not only save the gang but would also be the springboard for creating a republic. The oppression had reached the point where the victims felt they had few options but to fight back. They would then ride a wave of change with Ned at its head. Alex McDermott, on the other hand, thinks the extent of support from the sympathisers in the north-east has been greatly overstated. He believes the confrontation at Glenrowan represented more of a 'localised subculture of criminality rather than of political statement', and that the plot reflects a deep-rooted trait in Ned's personality. 'It shows that he's a man of extreme psychology in that questions of honour and prestige and status were almost literally a matter of life and death for him,' McDermott said.

The railwayman James Reardon was awoken by the sound of dogs barking at about twenty past two on the morning of the twenty-seventh. He left his small cottage to investigate and found his colleague Dennis Sullivan arriving on a horse, closely followed by Ned Kelly. Ned then pressed a revolver to Reardon's head and ordered his family out of the house. Reardon later told the Royal Commission that Ned made his intentions terrifyingly clear, even if he did stretch the truth:

> He [Kelly] said, 'I was in Beechworth last night and I had a great contract with the police, I have shot a lot of them, and I expect a train from Benalla with a lot of police and blackfellows, and I am going to kill all the b—'.

The only police Ned had shot were the three at Stringybark Creek twenty months earlier but again, it suited him to put a great fear into his hostages. Reardon begged to be left alone for the sake of his young family but Ned was having none of it. 'He then told me I had to tear up some rails or he would shoot me,' Reardon told the commission.

The railwayman had no choice but to accompany Ned to the embankment, where the rails were removed. Bravely, Reardon tried to foil Ned's plot at some risk to himself. He tried to convince Ned that removing just one length of line would do the trick but ended up removing two. Reardon later said that he removed 22 feet (6.7 metres) of line. He could have done the job in five minutes but stretched it out to an hour and a half. Secretly he hoped the train would jump the gap. Luckily for Reardon, it never came to that.

It was after four in the morning when the rails were finally lifted and dawn was just a few hours away. Ned must have felt relief that this difficult obstacle to the uprising had been overcome. By now Aaron Sherritt had been dead for nine hours and Ned calculated the police train was already steadily chugging its way north, or soon would be. What he could not have known was that, even as the rails were removed and cast aside, the police at Aaron's hut still had not raised the alarm. It would be another three hours before they mustered the courage to venture from the hut and more than ten hours before the police would even prepare to head for Kelly Country.

The outlaws took their prisoners back to the railway crossing at the Stanistreets' home. As the sun began to peep over the Warby Ranges to the east of Ann's hotel on the morning of Sunday the twenty-seventh, the police were still unaware of Sherritt's murder and the train was still at least fifteen hours from leaving Melbourne. It was then that Ann Jones made her first serious mistake. Sensing that the power had shifted to the Kellys she made a fateful offer. 'Come on up [to the inn], old man, have breakfast and a wash. You've been up all night, it'll refresh you.'

Ned refused the offer but moments later Ann repeated it. Ned looked over the railway line towards McDonnell's and then back towards Ann's pub. Then he made his decision. The Kellys and their hostages would go to Ann Jones' inn.

9

DISCOVERIES

'The turning point.'

There was a lot of media interest in the dig. A news day was held early in the project and there was a good turnout of reporters and camera crews. Following in the footsteps of Carrington, Madeley and the others, the journalists came to the siege site to see what they could add to the story. The reporters at the time of the siege had a wonderful new invention that enabled them to file their copy in record time. Soon after the events unfolded, words chattered down the telegraph line, where readers waited to devour them. In today's internet age, progress on the dig was posted online almost instantly but the principle remained the same. The public wanted to know about the Kellys and the reporters were there to tell them.

An ABC television crew followed the dig for a week and prepared a report for a current affairs program. Adam Ford was also in demand with radio talkback hosts and there was even interest from overseas news organisations. BBC radio ran an interview with Ford and the dig made online news at major

American newspapers. Local print, television and radio media followed the dig closely; the Kellys are always big news on their home turf and there was a voracious demand to see, photograph and film early discoveries at the site. The significance of the project was not lost on Albury-Wodonga's *The Border Mail*, which reported that a new chapter was being written in the Kelly story.

The media interest in the dig pales into insignificance, though, compared to the frenzy that engulfed Melbourne and Sydney in the hours after the siege. *The Daily Telegraph* reported in 1880 that it was impossible to walk along Collins Street in Melbourne because of a 'heaving, struggling mass of people, all clamorous for slips containing the news'. *The Age* said, 'there was never such excitement witnessed in Melbourne'. Newspapers rushed to print extra editions but still could not meet the demand and the crowds thronged the streets of Melbourne and Sydney till after nightfall.

The Kelly saga has been retold in each new medium invented. Storytelling was revolutionised forever early in the twentieth century with perhaps the most powerful medium of all—moving pictures. Some of the television news coverage of the dig in 2008 drew upon one of the earliest and most significant films ever shot—a film which nearly ended up being lost forever.

In 1906, *The Story of the Kelly Gang* was shot near Heidelberg in Melbourne. This silent black-and-white film is believed to be the world's first feature-length movie and was a sensation when it screened in Melbourne later that year. Demand to see it was so high that hundreds had to be turned away from the early screenings. It was not without controversy, especially in the north-east, where Ned's brother Jim tried to prevent it from being shown. Despite (or perhaps because of) the controversy, the film was a great commercial success in Australia and Britain, netting the producers an estimated £25,000. Even though it was shot twenty-six years after Ned's death, it is so realistic that many television news viewers today believe they are seeing film of the real thing. Unfortunately, though, only segments of the film survive—including one that was found on a Melbourne rubbish tip.

There have been many Kelly films since, including some early productions that were banned by censors, including 1922's *When the Kellys Rode*. In 1951, *The Glenrowan Affair* was filmed in Benalla and in the early 1970s Rolling Stone Mick Jagger was a rather strange choice to star in *Ned Kelly*—the first colour film made about the gang. When the film premiered at the Glenrowan Hall, a banner on the balcony of the town's pub announced: 'Welcome to the Republic of North Eastern Victoria. First President, Ned Kelly.' Ned would have liked that.

In 2008, the news media were shown some of the artefacts that had been recovered and Adam Ford answered questions about the dig. The Martini-Henry cartridges were useful exhibits for the cameras and the project got positive coverage in television, radio and newspapers. It was a good result for the government agencies coordinating the dig and helped to justify its cost.

The internet now meets much of the demand for information—both true and false—on the Kelly story. If you google Ned Kelly, you can get more than four million results in the time it takes to click a mouse. The widely read ironoutlaw.com site attracts between 250,000 and 300,000 individual visitors a year. Many of the visitors are Australian Kelly buffs or students doing research but others log on from all over the world. It is solid testimony to the power of the Kelly story in the silicon age. More than a century after the telegraph helped to kill off the last bushrangers, the internet is helping to keep them alive.

The second week of the dig seemed likely to end on a disappointing note. The data from the ground was still causing confusion and apart from the bullets and shells found earlier, there had been few discoveries of any significance. There was still a jigsaw of post holes to piece together, and the absence of artefacts indicated that the best might already have been found. Ford was still worried that the dig might appear to be something of a 'fizzer' from the public's point of view.

At least the weather was improving. As May draws on in Glenrowan, the long Indian summer finally loses its battle with autumn. The district had been baked dry in a decade-long drought, but May had hissed and spat with sudden cold showers as southerly winds gusted through, heralds of the big chill to come. The showers did little to ease the drought but plenty to turn the bottom of clean and structured trenches to mud. The wet weather did have a silver lining, as it had helped to define the post holes, making photographic recording a little easier, but at the same time it was a serious brake on progress. Time was running out and the team could not afford further delays.

On the morning of the twelfth day, the cold, grey showers had blown away, the sky seemed washed clean, and the sun was shining. The trenches were drying and the forecast was good. Ford had recovered his optimism:

Today is going to be the turning point because I reckon we're going to find the inn and I think we can find evidence of the first phase of occupation on the site. I'm pretty excited now.

The dig continued to attract a stream of tour buses, school groups and Kelly enthusiasts. On some days, Ford spent almost as much time addressing visitors as he did excavating the site. He developed a routine, firing imaginary shots from the front of the inn and ducking for cover from the return fire. It was popular with the kids and helped to show that the large, square trench in the ground was a gateway to a very human event in a very real place.

Such was the interest that some visitors returned several times to learn more and locals dropped in with interesting odds and ends. One man brought the remains of a revolver he said was found on the inn site years earlier. Another had the rusty barrel of a shotgun dragged from a farm dam. He wondered if it had been hidden there after the uprising failed. It prompted stories from older locals of rumours that multiple sets of Kelly armour had been made. They were said to be resting on the muddy bottom of a dam or spring, or in a stable, or buried in a farmer's paddock. Others told of secret stashes of gold hidden in the bush after the gang's bank raids. Tall tales for sure, but they did provide an intriguing window into the local folklore handed down through generations.

A couple from Wangaratta showed old black-and-white photos of the wine shanty. Two young blokes turned up wearing suits of armour over shorts and work boots. They watched the dig through the narrow slots of their helmets for a while

before clanking away. A man with a transparent image of Ned
Kelly on his car's rear windscreen parked in Siege Street and
watched the dig unfold for hours. Two middle-aged tourists
with well-behaved ferrets on leads stood on the viewing platform. Even the ferrets seemed interested in the work that was
taking place below. And all the while, the popping of recorded
gunshots rang out from the animated theatre that entertained
the tourists in the main street.

Frontal view of the dig. Image courtesy of Reece Rayner and Neal Kelly.

Among the visitors were a handful of people with very personal interests in the Kelly story. One was Anthony Griffiths,
a Greta resident who can claim direct lineage from Red and
Ellen Kelly. He is the great-grandson of Ned's youngest sister,
Grace, and speaks publicly about the family's history because he
knows people will discuss the Kellys with or without the family's
approval. He says he wants the family's version of the truth told.

Grace Kelly was just a teenager when Ned occupied Glenrowan and she survived the family's misfortunes, marrying Ned

Griffiths in 1889. Grace and Ned Griffiths moved around Victoria and New South Wales in the early years of their marriage and later returned to the north-east, where they moved into a wooden home at Greta. The house is still standing, but only just. Abandoned and leaning at a dangerous angle, it is home to possums and snakes and is hidden from the road by a screen of thick trees. From the modern-day Griffiths' point of view, the trees provided a welcome block to unwanted visitors. Such is the interest in the Kelly saga that visitors sometimes hop over barbed wire fences to poke around in the ruins of old buildings—not a practice welcomed by farmers.

The trees helped to keep the stickybeaks away from the old house, but there is not much left to see now anyway. Soon after the dig was completed, the house was battered by a summer storm and part of it collapsed into a pile of splintered timber and twisted iron. It was sad for those who saw the old home as one of the last tangible links to the Kelly family's pioneering days in Greta, but wooden buildings in the Kelly era were not made to last.

Anthony Griffiths gives well-considered answers to questions about the Kellys but the family pride and a residual sense of Irish injustice can be found in his responses. It is especially evident when the topic of police persecution is raised.

They [the Kelly family and friends] had their stock poisoned, their dogs were shot, horses stolen and yet they just kept on looking for justice and in the end they took the means for justice into their own hands—which wasn't that successful. But the personal qualities of the people involved—and not just Ned and his brother Dan, but the whole family—were remarkable. You look at the circumstances they were in—people today would just lie down and die.

Judith Douthie and Noeleen Lloyd were also among the visitors to the site. Judith did not expect to discover much more about her hostage ancestors but she hoped the ground would reveal more about the life and times of Ann Jones, and how the fight at the hotel affected not only those trapped in the pub but also the wider community. And she felt a lingering sense of sadness for the victims of the Last Stand:

My family's lives changed because of the events but it was a great loss to Noeleen's family as well as the end of a dream . . . yeah, a great loss.

Adam Ford's optimism proved to be well founded. On the thirteenth day, soil was brushed away from the area that was believed to be Ann's dining room, revealing a long rectangle of black ash. It became clear that this was the charred remains of a floor joist in the right place and context to have come from the hotel. The ash sat directly on the ground, indicating that the joist had supported Ann Jones' floorboards until they were consumed by the fire that destroyed the inn. With a risk of showers returning, the team had to work quickly to investigate and record the find. This discovery did not have the glamour of the artefacts that were still to be drawn from the ground but for the archaeologists it was of great significance. It meant that traces of Ann Jones' inn still survived and it would help them piece together the mysterious jigsaw of post holes.

A rethink on how to interpret the posts finally provided a breakthrough. Ford and Sterenberg drew a floor plan of the inn on a whiteboard and then boarded a cherry picker to gain a bird's eye view of the excavation. This made it easier to differentiate the post holes of the original inn from those of later buildings. The shape and size of the inn was starting to become clear. Ian Jones helped to provide the next clue by showing Ford Madeley's photographs taken of the pub before it caught fire. Using a ruler to measure the scale, Jones and Ford were able to get a better understanding of the building they were looking for.

Measuring up. An old photograph and a ruler help to solve a knotty problem. Courtesy Reece Rayner and Neal Kelly.

The key lay in understanding just how small Ann's hotel was. On the outside at least, it was little more than a bush shack. A comparison of the photograph with the post holes revealed it was only about 11 metres wide and about 8 metres deep, including the bedrooms at the back. This was a building smaller than a modern home unit and at the height of the drama it contained more than forty terrified people. This interpretation helped to paint a mental picture of the cramped and bloody conditions during the siege as men, women and children jostled for cover from the bullets.

More importantly for the archaeologists, it enabled an accurate assessment of exactly where the building had stood. Ford now hoped to find the remains of the eastern and western fire-places to nail down the entire layout of the inn. With a new approach and some patient trowel work he soon had one of the lost fireplaces, or thought he did. The bricks from Ann's hearths had been taken up and probably re-used in a later building but, at the eastern end of the inn, a fireplace had left a faint signature. This was a pinkish stain left in the ground by super-heated bricks. Tiny studs of charring in the pink soil proved it had been part of a fireplace and the team speculated it was the hearth in the dining room—the scene of so much jollity on the final day of the building's existence.

To the team's disappointment, it was later established that the hearth stains probably came from a later construction on the site, most likely the second hotel built by Ann Jones. Adam Ford had hoped the original inn would have had a stone base for the hearth but there was no sign of it. Neither was there any sign of an earlier fireplace. He later came to the view that the original fireplace had been dug out and the stone base never existed. 'I think the fireplaces were built directly onto the earth and there were no stone foundations,' he said. 'They were pretty jerry-built and I think the bricks were removed quite soon after the fire, before Ann Jones' second building was put up.'

So, while the fireplace proved to be misleading, it did focus attention on that part of the site and the investigation there helped to establish the line of the eastern wall. A jagged stump of wood in a hole provided the breakthrough. When the post hole was cleaned out it showed the post had been erected onto virgin natural soil, meaning it had to be part of the original inn. Because it was a large, load-bearing post, the team could be sure it was one of the main supports for the roof on the eastern wall. The fireplace might have been lost but the broken stump could be lined up with other post holes to clearly establish the eastern wall of Ann Jones' inn. Even though the fireplace was gone, the team could now say for certain where Ann's customers would have stood as they warmed their hands next to the dining room fire.

The second hearth—in the tiny parlour at the western end of the hotel—was also lost. Whatever traces it left were probably dug out when the wine shanty was built, as both buildings shared a common boundary on the western side. Further damage may have been done by the later installation of underground services along the Beaconsfield Parade footpath. In fact, the entire western end of Ann Jones' inn—the part that was set alight by the police in 1880—had ceased to exist. But all was not lost. The establishment of the eastern edge, and analysis of more post holes, soon enabled Ford and the team to map out two of the four exterior walls, as well as the front verandah posts. When the post holes for the two bedrooms were confirmed at the rear of the pub, the team suddenly had three sides of the inn. It was a great relief. 'I'm so glad we've got it now and to really have the original inn, never seen before, fully exposed and fully recorded and hopefully fully understood is really exciting,' Ford said.

The dig was now a success in archaeological terms. But it had come at a cost because unravelling the complexity of the jumbled-up site had taken longer than expected. The project was behind schedule and the inn still had not been fully excavated. With less than two weeks left, Adam Ford had to make a decision; he had to abandon his hopes of excavating the entire site and concentrate solely on the inn itself. There would be no time to search for Ann's cesspits, the holes where she dumped the inn's rubbish. This waste from the inn would have provided some fascinating clues to the life and times of the people living there in that brief period at the end of the 1870s but the rubbish pits would have to remain untapped. The stables at the rear of the site might also have provided more information about Glenrowan during Kelly times. They, too, remain unexcavated.

But the biggest disappointment was the lost chance to excavate the kitchen and humble home of Ann Jones and her six children. A tantalising glimpse of the building had been found in a line of square post holes just behind the rear of the inn. These square holes were the oldest on the site and clear evidence of the front wall of the residence. It showed that at least part of the kitchen and residence survived, but, frustratingly, there would be no time to excavate it. Whatever else is left of Ann's home still remains under the ground. Until it too is unearthed, one of the most sensational fables of the Kelly Gang—that Dan Kelly and Steve Hart survived the siege—will refuse to die.

10

A DATE WITH DESTINY

'I am sorry, but I must detain you.'

Thomas Curnow's schoolhouse was a small, L-shaped weatherboard building to the west of the inn. It was moved in the 1890s—well after Thomas left town in a hurry—and incorporated into the new school that was built nearby. This is where the district's primary school children are taught today. There have been many teachers in the town over the generations—some of them no doubt fine educators of young people—but only one of them became infamous. Thomas Curnow is remembered as committing an act of treachery and, sure enough, he did. But he was also a brave man and, whether he acted for reward or on moral principle, he saved many lives.

Thomas' date with destiny began with a carriage ride through the rough streets of Glenrowan on the morning of 27 June 1880. It seemed like any other Sunday morning to Thomas, as he and his pregnant wife, Jean, his sister, Catherine, and Jean's nineteen-year-old brother, David Mortimer, clip-clopped along the unpaved roads. Jean nursed the couple's baby, Muriel, and David Mortimer rode alongside the gig on a horse. Thomas first got an inkling that something was wrong when he rode past Ann's hotel and noticed a crowd gathered at the railway gate. His first thought was a gloomy one. 'Mrs Jones must be dead,' he said to his companions. 'She has been very ill.'

Thomas drove past the hotel to the railway gate at the Stanistreet home. There he met John Stanistreet, who announced, 'The Kellys are here; you can't get through.' Thomas thought the stationmaster was joking but nobody laughed because then a man on horseback wheeled the horse around and announced, 'I am sorry, but I must detain you.' Ever so politely, Ned Kelly had taken hostage the man who would be his undoing some eighteen hours later.

Thomas had a pronounced limp because of a hip abnormality and he has sometimes been depicted in film as a hobbling, almost sinister character. In real life, he was rather handsome. His photograph shows a high-foreheaded man with a neat beard and a resolute gaze. The son of a Cornish copper miner, Thomas had been living at Glenrowan for four years and had done well to rise from his family's working-class background in the old country. But Australians hate a dobber and Thomas was the biggest dobber of them all. After the siege, he was constantly fearful for his safety. He later told of his secret life under a new name in the 'wilds of Gippsland', and of threats made against him, but he never regretted his actions at Glenrowan.

Thomas and his family were made to enter the Stanistreet home, where they learned almost the entire town had been 'stuck up' by Ned and his gang. The number of hostages had now risen to about sixty men, women and children. Thomas quickly discovered that the rail lines had been ripped up and that Ned intended to wreck the train. Soon, the schoolmaster would plot ways of averting the catastrophe but in the meantime he was left in no doubt about Ned's feelings for the police. Thomas later told the Royal Commission:

> Ned Kelly declared to all of us who were listening to him that he would have the life of anyone who aided the police in any way, or who even showed a friendly feeling for them, and declared that he could and would find them out. He said that a law was made rendering it a crime for anyone to help . . . [the outlaws] . . . and that he would make it a crime against the Kelly Gang for anyone to aid the police.

So, Ned was already making up laws to suit himself. His republic had not even been born but he was already becoming presidential. He decided to make his point using a young hostage named John Delaney. In Ned's eyes, Delaney had committed the serious offence of wanting to join the police. This would not have been a good career move in Ned Kelly's republic and Ned made blood-curdling threats to the young man. Thomas later said Ned 'kept Delaney in extreme terror for about half an hour'. Young John was so frightened that he crushed the stem of his pipe between his teeth. The women hostages pleaded for Delaney's life and Ned let him off the hook. 'I forgive you this time; but mind you be careful for the future,' the bushranger said. He also extracted a promise that Delaney would abandon thoughts of a career in uniform.

Thomas later admitted that Ned's attack on nineteen-year-old Delaney was just for show. The Delaneys of Greta were supporters of the Kellys and Ned's outburst might have been directed at Curnow and the other hostages rather than at poor John Delaney. Ned might also have been laying a smokescreen to protect the Delaneys against retaliation. Whatever the motive, the attack was effective. At the time, Thomas Curnow must have believed that Ned would indeed fulfil his threat of murder.

Fifteen-year-old Thomas Cameron was already a prisoner by the time the Curnows arrived at the railway crossing. That morning Tom had been to the Reardons' home and was surprised to find nobody there. He had joined up with John Delaney to search for the missing Reardons when they, too, had run into Ned Kelly and were taken prisoner. In a letter to his brother in July 1880, Tom wrote that he met Joe Byrne riding between the Stanistreet and Reardon homes. Joe decided that young Tom would benefit from a nip of brandy. 'I didn't want to at first but he made me,' wrote Tom. 'We were knocking about there all day, but we couldn't escape because they kept too sharp an eye on us.' Young Tom talked for 'a long time' with Joe, and it was Joe who told the young prisoner about the rails being torn up and the plan to kill the police and black trackers.

'But what they wanted to do was too bad,' observed Tom.

It had been a stressful, sleepless night for Ned and as the morning of the twenty-seventh progressed he had to deal with the problem of keeping an entire town hostage. It was becoming rather unwieldy and there was a risk somebody could escape and raise the alarm. It was a difficult balancing act to keep control of so many people but Ned was no stranger to holding up entire towns. In fact, he was rather good at it.

After Stringybark Creek, the gang had fled in the hope of escaping into New South Wales. They had ridden north in torrential rain as rivers and creeks broke their banks and when they reached the Murray it was a lake of surging floodwater. They sought help at the home of William Baumgarten, who had allegedly been involved in the Kellys' horse-stealing racket. But William's wife, Margaret, alerted the police that the gang was in the district. There was no way across the swollen Murray and with the police on their tail, the gang hid in a bed of dense reeds. With their firearms soaked and their horses exhausted, their exploits could have ended here but they survived—the police did not see them in the downpour.

Now there was no choice but to turn back for a lonely, hunted ride back into the heart of their country. While the Kelly Gang headed south, looking for a place to cross the swollen Ovens River and so escape into the Warby Ranges, the police charged into the Woolshed Valley in a noisy cavalcade of horses and men. Acting on a tip (actually a drunken message from a bark stripper at a Beechworth hotel) they raided the homes of supporters, including Aaron Sherritt's father and Joe Byrne's mother. It caused a terrible ruckus and prompted the press to dub the escapade 'The Great Sebastopol Raid', but it did not find a trace of the gang.

Less than a week later, a deadline for the Kellys to surrender expired. On 15 November 1878, the gang was outlawed and could now be taken dead or alive. Ned's mother, Ellen, was in prison, the homes of their supporters had been raided and their friends would be turned against them. It was too late to go back. Ned would lead the gang in an exploit that was already going beyond banditry and evolving into a crude plan for a political solution. Ned aimed to restore his name and free his mother from prison, at the same time demanding that the wrongs against his family and friends be righted. To do that, he would need money.

The best place to get money was a bank. Ned decided the National Bank in Euroa, a sleepy village north of Melbourne, could be relieved of its funds at gunpoint. No ordinary stick-up, it was a carefully planned and executed operation that not only provided money for the gang and their friends, but was also the first big shot in Ned's propaganda war with the authorities. If he was to achieve more than outlawry he would have to make a statement and, thanks to a parliamentarian named Donald Cameron, that statement would be made at Euroa. Cameron had raised the matter of the Kelly outbreak in parliament and, wrongly thinking that Cameron was an ally, Ned took a pot of red ink to Euroa, where he and Joe Byrne—the best educated of the gang—wrote a letter to the politician.

The Cameron Letter was a shorter version of the more famous Jerilderie Letter. Both contained a powerful defence of Ned's actions and also included warnings that Ned would fight back if his demands were not met. But the letter to the politician ended with an offer of peace and a warning.

> . . . if I get justice, I will cry a go [give up bushranging].
> For I need no lead or power
> To avenge my cause,
> And if words be louder,
> I will oppose your laws

With no offence (and remember your railroads),
     and a sweet goodbye from
Edward Kelly, a forced outlaw.

Sadly for Ned, the Cameron Letter was not fully published in his lifetime. One copy was sent to the politician and another to the police superintendent John Sadleir. Cameron never read out the letter in the House and although segments of it were published in the newspapers, most of it was suppressed. Strangely, though, the remarkable events that took place in Euroa proved to be something of a public relations victory for the gang, mainly due to the extraordinary qualities of their leader.

On the afternoon of Monday 9 December, the Kelly Gang rode openly to Faithfull's Creek Station on the outskirts of town. Soon, fourteen men were bailed up and held prisoner in a shed. Not one to pass up an opportunity to air his grievances, Ned regaled his captives with his story. It was on that night that he first spoke of his intention to 'overturn a train' if his imprisoned mother was not given justice. He spoke of the shootings at Stringybark Creek, excusing his brother and friends of blame but also denying charges of murder. 'The . . . papers call me a murderer but I never murdered anyone in my life,' he said. Of the killing of Kennedy, he said it had been a fair fight and he wished Kennedy had surrendered.

On the following morning, the gang rode to the National Bank, where they bailed up the manager, Robert Scott, and his wife, Susan. Scott tried to stall Ned's demands for cash by claiming he could not find the keys to the safe. Luckily, perhaps, for the brave bank manager, it was his wife who delivered the keys to Ned—and with them some £2,260 in cash, bullion and bank sureties. Mrs Scott was quite taken with the rugged bush-ranger. When told to prepare for a journey, she changed into her best finery. This must have raised eyebrows around the room, especially, one imagines, those of her husband. But the bank manager was a forgiving type because almost two years later at Ned's murder trial he would say: 'The prisoner [Ned] treated me personally very well.' He also noted that Ned 'did not use a single rude word to Mrs Scott'. The lady herself was more effusive. Ned was 'much more handsome and well dressed . . . than I had expected . . . and by no means the ferocious ruffian I imagined him to be'.

Ned was already well on the way towards winning the hearts and minds of the people. The gang, with the robbery takings and a party of hostages in tow, set off back to Faithfull's Creek Station. The wife of the town's stationmaster observed the group passing by and thought it was the 'bank people with a lot of friends going off for a picnic'. And it was a festive atmosphere as the gang rounded off the robbery in style. Robert Scott asked Ned where he and his men would go. Ned replied, 'Oh, the country belongs to us; we can go any road we like.'The Kellys then thrilled the townsfolk with a display of horseback skills before leaping over a fence and vanishing into the gathering dusk.

The gang now had pockets full of money (although less than the £10,000 Ned had expected) and a small victory in the propaganda war. Although the red-inked Cameron Letter was not printed in full, the tide of hostile press for the gang seemed to abate after the Euroa robbery. If the press retained its vitriol for the Kellys, it at least turned some of its attack back on the police. *The Argus* sniffed:

That they [the Kellys] have outwitted the police is obvious, and until some explanation is given, the public cannot fail to hold the opinion that an outrage has been perpetrated which ought to have been prevented.

The Ovens and Murray Advertiser was no fan of the gang but noted that 'the exploits of other knights of the road pale into insignificance' compared to the adventure at Euroa. The *Advertiser* also could not help but admire the generalship of Ned Kelly and observed that the police pursuit of the gang had been 'a bungle from start to finish'. And proving that interstate rivalry is not a new thing, *The Sydney Morning Herald* noted that New South Wales police held a low opinion of their Victorian counterparts. A Thomas Carrington drawing in *Melbourne Punch* depicted Ned Kelly sitting in the premier's chair. An avid consumer of his own press, Ned must have been delighted with this last effort. More than that, it might have encouraged him to seek a political solution to his problems.

Soon, cash was flowing through the north-east as dirt-poor Kelly sympathisers suddenly found themselves flush with funds. Ned had not only pulled off a remarkable stunt worthy of a ballad of Robin Hood, he had backed it up by robbing the rich to give to the poor. But his war was only just beginning. Two months later, he held up the New South Wales village of Jerilderie—an isolated outpost that would give its name to one of the most significant documents in Australian history.

Within days of the Euroa 'outrage' the homes of sympathisers were raided and many arrested in an ill-advised move that simply generated more support for the outlaws. The reward on the Kellys' heads increased. Rumours spread that they would again try to flee across the Murray into New South Wales. This story was probably put about by Aaron Sherritt, who told police that the gang was headed for Goulburn. The story was close enough to the truth for Sherritt to retain the trust of the police as an informer but inaccurate enough to add weight to the case for Aaron as a double agent. As speculation built, huge police resources were brought to bear on Kelly Country and the press bayed for results. The gang was seen everywhere and found nowhere. In fact, they were hiding out with Tom Lloyd and other supporters near Greta.

The editor of the *Jerilderie and Urana Gazette*, Samuel Gill, wrote that his under-policed town could be a target for the Kellys. In doing so, he provided a blueprint showing how to hold the town hostage and rob its banks, including information on where the outlaws could safely cross the Murray River. It is not known if Ned read Gill's articles but if not, it is remarkably coincidental that Jerilderie was held up in much the same way as the editor had expected.

Jerilderie is a small oasis on the hot and dusty plains of the southern Riverina. The land is flat and vast, broken by Australia's longest creek—the Billabong Creek—and crossed by a network of canals that pump the lifeblood of water into this semi-arid settlement. Its main industry is irrigation farming but the events that took place there in February 1879 have ensured its place on the Kelly tourist route.

Jerilderie is proud of its heritage. Regulars in the front bar of a main street pub were once asked whether they thought Ned Kelly was hero or villain. 'A bloody hero, mate,' said one blue-singleted bloke. 'He only robbed the bloody bank, you know.'

'Yeah,' chimed in the blue-singleted one's mate, a farm worker in a cap, 'and the fuckin' banks have been robbing us ever since!'

The raid on Jerilderie started on 7 February 1879 when the gang rode to a hotel about two miles from the town. They called in for a drink to test public feelings about themselves and were pleased to hear praise for the gang from the barmaid. She even sang them a ballad about the exploits of the Kellys. The following night, a Saturday, the gang began to seize control of the town. At about midnight, the town's police were roused from bed to hear the dreaded words: 'I'm Kelly. Put up your hands.' The police station was then secured, along with the officers and their families. The pregnant wife of Constable Devine was among the hostages and she was another to fall for Ned's charms. The next morning, Ned emptied a tub of bathwater for her, saying it was not a job for her, 'in her condition'. In *A Short Life*, Ian Jones notes that Mrs Devine would later privately describe Ned as 'the kindest man I ever met'.

Soon the gang was dressed in stolen police uniforms. Keen to establish an air of normality, Dan Kelly helped Mrs Devine decorate the church with flowers for the Sunday service. The gang then spent the day scoping out the town, caring for their horses and cleaning their weapons. Most of the townsfolk were unaware that the most infamous men in the land were among them, disguised as police. Ned's men had already robbed the rich to give to the poor; now they had enacted another Robin Hood legend by wearing the uniforms of their enemies. That afternoon, Joe dropped in to the pub to catch up with a gloriously named barmaid, Mary the Larrikin, while Ned filled in the day reading to Mrs Devine from a wad of papers. The policeman's wife later remembered none of the letter's contents and could not have known she was hearing a first-hand rendition of the document that came to be known as the Jerilderie Letter.

This was a reworked version of the unpublished Cameron Letter, and in it Ned Kelly (with Joe's help) had voiced his grievances, his rage and his warnings. Part manifesto, part litany of excuses, the letter described Ned's hatred for the police and his fury at the treatment of his family and friends. It ranted in anger and argued with reason. It contained a confession to killing the police at Stringybark Creek but vehemently justified it as self-defence. The letter expressed Ned's fury at being forced outside the law by police dishonesty and corruption. It demanded justice for the poor and oppressed and dished out magnificent abuse to his many enemies. And it left no doubt that Ned would fight back.

> It will pay the Government to give those people who are suffering innocence, justice and liberty. If not I will be compelled to show some colonial stratagem which will open the eyes of not only the Victorian Police and inhabitants, but also the whole British Army.

Fitzpatrick, the policeman who had started it all, came in for special mention. Ned warned that Fitzpatrick would 'be the cause of greater slaughter to the Union Jack than St Patrick was to the snakes and toads in Ireland'. The long and barely punctuated letter ended with the chilling statement, 'I am a widow's son outlawed and my orders must be obeyed.'

The letter has been praised as a soaring manifesto and also criticised as an immature rant. The anti-Kelly writer, Christopher Bantick, described it as 'a long discursive piece of utter tripe'.

Alex McDermott, however, who cannot be regarded as a member of Ned's cheer squad, wrote in his book about the letter:

> Even now it's hard to defy his voice. With this letter Kelly inserts himself into history, on his own terms with his own voice . . . it is one of the most extraordinary documents in Australian history.

It was Ned's intention to have the letter printed in the Jerilderie newspaper office for wide distribution but the editor—the same Mr Gill who had warned of the threat to the town—fled when news of the hold-up became known. Copies were made but the letter remained unpublished until more than fifty years after Ned's death. It was another warning that went unheeded. And for the unfortunate editor, it would go down as a remarkable opportunity lost. Gill could have published the letter and scored the scoop of a lifetime but his healthy instinct for self-preservation cost him that chance.

The next day, the gang spent a leisurely Monday robbing the bank, helping themselves to more than £2000. Many of the townsfolk were now held hostage. In a preview of what would take place at Glenrowan some sixteen months later, Ned took his prisoners to the pub and bought them a drink. It must have been a jolly time, although Joe Byrne might have been a little hung-over. During his dalliance with Mary the Larrikin on the previous day, he got so drunk that he had to be helped onto his horse. The gang left town the next day and remained at large until the next—and last—time they took a town hostage.

And so Ned felt quite well equipped to handle the business of mass hold-ups. But as the morning of Sunday 27 June 1880 passed, it seemed he might have taken on more than he could cope with. Most of Glenrowan was now under his control and he had dozens of prisoners to manage. Only the policeman Hugh Bracken remained free, perhaps because Ned knew Bracken had the flu and was confined to the barracks where the postmaster, a sympathiser named Hillmorton Reynolds, could keep an eye on him. Most of the women and children were now being kept at the Stanistreets' home under the watchful eye of Steve Hart and the men had been taken to Ann Jones' pub. The gang made sure nobody could escape and Ned frequently threatened to shoot anyone who tried.

Some were there in fear of their lives, others were neutral and a few were even there by choice. During the day, the gang added to the list of 'hostages' by rounding up the publican Paddy McDonnell, his wife, Hanorah, and other sympathisers. This was just for show as the McDonnells were integral members of the plot. The gang had earlier visited McDonnell's pub under codenames and seen to it that their horses and drum of blasting powder were safe under the McDonnells' care. Paddy was free to come and go as he wished and might even have wandered home to get his dinner.

The smokescreen worked from the McDonnells' point of view because they escaped retribution, although they could have tried a little harder to throw off any suspicions. Mrs McDonnell later told a newspaper of jokes and laughs with the bushrangers after she and her family were 'rounded up'. 'I at once recognised Ned Kelly and said, "Oh, Ned, how altered you are." He said, "Don't call me Ned. My name is Jack Hoyle," and then they all laughed,' she said.

Steve Hart was going by the name of Collie, she said, and Joe was called Sugar 'because he was so sweet on the girls'. They had a drink and a cheery conversation with the McDonnells before Ned took them all over to Ann's pub. 'The outlaws were very civil and joked and laughed with us constantly,' Mrs McDonnell said.

Other key members of the plot were nearby but staying out of sight. They possibly even raised a glass to Ned and the gang from the safety of McDonnell's that afternoon. Ned's cousin Jack Lloyd (Jnr) and Jack's older brother Tom, who was known as 'the fifth Kelly', were among those waiting for the call to arms. So, too, was Wild Wright, the man Ned once beat in a brutal bare-knuckle fight. We will probably never know, but Jim Kelly might have been there as well. If so, he got clear in time. After the siege, Jim mostly stayed out of trouble, never married and lived to a ripe old age.

The McAuliffe brothers, Denis and Patrick, arrived at the inn to be made prisoners, which was very cooperative of them, given that they had only just come from caring for the gang's horses at McDonnell's. The McAuliffes were among the staunchest of Kelly supporters. As descendants of transported convicts, the family had much in common with the Kellys, having struggled equally under their colonial masters. It is possible the youngest McAuliffe, the teenaged George Thomas, was at the inn as well.

George's grandson, Max McAuliffe, began asking about the events of June 1880 some sixty years ago. Even well into the twentieth century the scars from the uprising were painful and, for many, it was a taboo topic. For some it still is. When Max first asked his father for information about his family's part in the siege, he was told to keep quiet and mind his own business. An uncle would only say, 'You'll find out some day.' Max did eventually find out and now he tells a handed-down story of Ned confronting the young George Thomas at the inn, saying: 'What are you doing here, young McAuliffe? You'd best get under the table.' Max does not know if his grandfather took Ned's advice but George survived the siege—if he was ever there—so perhaps he had the good sense to duck for cover once the bullets started flying. Max McAuliffe—who grew up in the north-east but now lives in Melbourne—also tells of a secret cave used as a mail drop for the Kellys and a hidden hut in the Greta Swamp where the gang could find friends and food. And he says the McAuliffes remain Kelly supporters 130 years later: 'I think it's what he stood for, which was to try and get a fairer time for the battlers.'

So, after lunch on the twenty-seventh Ned was in control of Glenrowan. But still there was no sign of the police train and time was passing. With a group of restless prisoners gathered at the pub and a long wait likely, Ned did what any self-respecting Irish-Australian would do. He decided to hold a party.

11
CELLAR MYSTERY

'I'm the real Dan Kelly'

Few people were more disappointed to learn that Ann's home and kitchen would not be excavated than Maureen Tyler, a grandmother from Toowoomba in Queensland. In the second week of the dig, she made the 1500-kilometre journey to Glenrowan in the hope of finding answers to a family mystery—her grandfather, Charles Devine Tindall, had quietly claimed to be the real Dan Kelly.

Charles Tindall told only one person of his alleged secret, his son Stan, who passed it on to his children. Charles had said he and Steve Hart had hidden in the cellar at Ann Jones' inn during the fire and escaped after the siege. They went to Queensland, where they split up and spent the rest of their lives under false names. Charles revealed almost nothing else about his youth but when he died he left a leather-covered prayer book with 'D. Kelly' scrawled on a page in indelible pencil.

Charles Tindall had burns on his side, which he claimed to have suffered while hiding in Ann's cellar. He never sought publicity and never attempted to make money from his story. The Tindall family looked into his past but could find no records of his birth, his parents or his childhood. He was a small man, about 1.7 metres tall. Dan Kelly was also of small stature. Maureen Tyler says her grandfather was not a braggart and she cannot understand why he would have told his story if it was not true. She hoped the dig at Glenrowan would uncover the fabled cellar to add weight to Charles' story.

Whoever he was, Charles Devine Tindall was secretive. Maureen Tyler said:

He used to get his mail from the train station and he'd read it, then he'd burn it. And it was always addressed to Mr *Dan* Tindall. He said it was from his sister, Kate He would never have a photo taken and there were only two that remain, and they didn't come to light until he died.

Charles Tindall's secrets died with him in 1953, when he was probably aged in his nineties. If Dan Kelly had lived, he would have turned ninety-two in that year.

After the siege, two bodies were recovered from the western bedrooms of the inn. They were charred to cinders. A rather gruesome photograph by John Bray shows one of the bodies laid out on a sheet of bark, its limbs burned away and the torso just a blackened stump. It was impossible to identify either body but, strangely, the police almost immediately released the remains to the Kelly family, rather than retaining the bodies for an inquest. Supporters of the survival theory point to this decision as evidence that the police knew Dan and Steve were still alive but did not want to be blamed for another failure to capture them.

One of the burned bodies lying on a sheet of bark, 29 June 1880. Photographer John Bray. Image courtesy of the Pictures Collection, State Library of Victoria.

The survival theory was given weight by Ned himself, who said as he lay wounded at the Glenrowan railway station that 'the boys' had got away. The Royal Commission also heard of concerns that two of the outlaws had fled the inn. But Ned had also said that Joe Byrne had escaped. There is no dispute that Joe was shot dead at the bar of the inn, so was the grievously wounded Ned confused? Or was he trying to cover for his mates?

Ned's misleading statement, combined with the doubt about the identities of the bodies, fuelled the stories that Dan and Steve survived and that two swagmen at the inn had been the true victims of the fire. Soon after the siege, reports emerged that the bushrangers were shearing in western New South Wales, droving in Queensland or even fighting in the Boer War. In 1901, a Sydney journalist named William Melville wrote of meeting two men who claimed to be the real Dan Kelly and Steve Hart in Pretoria, South Africa. Melville described them as 'two men of middle age, athletic, keen-eyed, sunburnt, grim-featured—typical Australian bushmen'.

They told the reporter that they had survived the gunfight and that the two swagmen had been shot dead. ('Two drunken coves was shot dead through the winder.') 'Dan' and 'Steve' claimed they escaped by donning police uniforms and slipping out of the pub, firing shots back into the building as cover while they fled into the darkness. They said they eventually went to Sydney and then to South Africa, where they fought the Boers.

It was a ripping yarn—and completely false.

None of the police at Glenrowan wore uniforms and none of the hostages ever reported seeing the Kellys with uniforms as disguises. If anyone had worn a police uniform at the Glenrowan siege he would instantly have stood out as an impostor, so the story can be dismissed. There is nothing to say why the 'grim-featured bushmen' spun their yarn to the reporter and we can only guess they were indulging in the great Australian tradition of taking the mickey. But they were not Dan and Steve.

Claimants to be the real Dan Kelly and the real Steve Hart continued to emerge, mostly in Queensland. John Harris, a farmer from the Brisbane Valley near Ipswich, remembers an old hermit who lived in a little shack near the Harris farm in the 1930s and 40s. That man, James Ryan, claimed to be Dan Kelly. In 1933, Ryan told a newsreel crew: 'I'm the real Dan

Kelly, brother of Ned Kelly who was hanged in 1880. I was meant to have died in the Glenrowan fire.'

The grainy black-and-white footage shows the bearded vagrant defying his critics to believe him. 'Well, you people may judge me for yourself if I'm dead or not. I'll tell you how I got out of the fire with flames throughout the building.'

Ryan—who had burn scars on his back and the initials DK branded on a buttock—took the story of how he 'escaped' to the sideshow circuit during the Depression years. In 1948, at the age of eighty-four, he was hit and killed by a train. He was buried at the Ipswich cemetery and a plaque inscribed with the Kelly armour marks his grave. A small sign explains that some believe Ryan's grave could actually be that of Dan Kelly. The theory is promoted by an influential Ipswich City councillor, Paul Tully. He says Ryan's story could never be shaken and wants the Victorian coroner to hold an inquest into the deaths of Dan and Steve. But for John Harris, it is more personal. He says: 'If the story is true then I would probably be the only person alive who could say they sat on Dan Kelly's lap as a child.'

There are also candidates for the real Steve Hart. In the Queensland town of Murgon, an old horse breaker named Billy Meade spoke his dying words to a matron at a hospital. He said he had been living a lie and was really the infamous bushranger. Like Steve, Meade was slight of build and was good with horses but his past is a blank page. His story intrigued local people, even inspiring a bush ballad telling of the wanted men's desperate flight into exile. In 2007, meetings were held in a country hall near Murgon to discuss Billy Meade. It was hoped that someone in the district would have enough knowledge of his history to at least establish whether his Hart claim bore investigation. Almost nothing came to light. Billy Meade seemed to have been around forever but nobody knew where he had come from.

It was also said that two shearers who knew Dan Kelly before Glenrowan later saw him working in northern New South Wales. Then there were tales of a silent bushman—another Dan Kelly—who always sat facing the door with a pistol on his lap. There were other Steve Harts, too, including a man named Fred Layton who is buried near Roma in Queensland. Layton was described as the spitting image of Steve Hart.

One veteran Kelly researcher believes it is likely that Ann Jones' inn did have a cellar and that two men may well have hidden there during the fire. Gary Dean is the owner of the Cobb & Co museum in Glenrowan and with another Kelly expert, Dagmar Balcarek, has co-written several Kelly books. During his studies, Dean became interested in family lore that told of a cellar, 'three foot by three foot by four' with a heavy steel lid. He found consistent accounts of two men hiding in the cellar as the inn burnt and escaping at nightfall. He also believes Jim Kelly travelled to Queensland after the siege, a long journey and one without any apparent purpose other than to see his brother. It all fitted with documented evidence from Ned that Dan and Steve survived the fire.

Muddying the waters somewhat, Gary Dean believes Charles Devine Tindall was one of the men hiding in the cellar but he does not believe Tindall was Dan Kelly. Dean believes that a man named Jack Day, who regularly sent money from Queensland to Greta, was the true Dan Kelly. 'There was money every fortnight,' Dean said. 'Jack would go to the nearest post office and put half his wage in an envelope and it was usually addressed to Jim Kelly, care of the Glenrowan Post Office.' A photo of Day revealed a powerful likeness to Dan Kelly.

One of the first steps towards establishing whether Day or Tindall—or any of the other claimants—was telling the truth would be to determine whether there was a cellar at the inn.

Gary Dean worked as a volunteer on the inn excavation. Although it quickly became clear that there was no cellar under the front rooms of the inn, he began to wonder about a square of concrete over the area of the western bedroom—the very place where the charred bodies of two people were found after the fire. Roughly two metres by two metres, the twentieth-century concrete slab appeared to be a lid over a depression in the ground. Adam Ford called in the excavator to break up the slab. If it masked a hidden cellar, it would be instantly clear to the archaeologists. When the concrete was removed, however, all that was left was a shallow, gravel-filled bowl. Clearly, it was not a cellar.

It could be said with certainty that there had been no cellar below the five rooms of the inn but that did not mean there was no cellar at all. If there was one, then it may have been under the kitchen—the oldest building on the site and the most obvious place to store perishable food. The inability of the dig to rule a cellar in or out leaves open the tantalising possibility that there was indeed an amazing escape. It is a story that is nearly as old as the siege itself and it has a powerful persistence. It has always bubbled away, sometimes following different paths, but usually returning to the core elements of cellar, flight and Queensland. Truth can be stranger than fiction and it is possible to imagine

Dan and Steve huddled at the bottom of Ann's cellar as her home burned above them. We could see them spirited away by night, cared for and protected by friends until finally they could slip away into the outback anonymity of life as Aussie bushmen. It would be a secretive and lonely life and with the threat of a rope around their necks there could be no return. Because the story keeps occurring it is worth examining.

The first person to see the bodies in the bedroom was the Western Australian Catholic priest Father Mathew Gibney. One of the bravest men in the Kelly story, he was travelling by rail through Glenrowan on 28 June when he heard about the siege. He learned there was no Catholic priest there and decided to see if he could save lives or souls. He arrived at about midday, by which time most of the hostages had been released, but Dan and Steve were still holding the police at bay. By then, Ned had been captured and was lying wounded in the stationmaster's office. Gibney was able to see him there and asked if it was safe to broker a truce. Ned said it was not, 'as his comrades might shoot without stopping to think'. Soon after that, the police decided to set fire to the inn. As *The Argus* later reported, the priest was horrified.

> When the house was fired his feelings revolted. He wished . . . the building might not take fire . . . and thought that was his time to go to the hotel as he believed the outlaws would be glad of any truce.

The police ordered Gibney to stand back but he defied them. He broke free and ran through the fire zone and onto the verandah. The flames were taking hold and smoke filled the inn as he burst through the dining room door and into the bar. He found the armour-clad body of Joe Byrne at the entrance to the passageway, next to the counter where he had taken his last drink. The grievously wounded Irishman Martin Cherry was barely conscious in the kitchen. In the bedroom Gibney found two bodies, lying side by side on the beds with pillows under their heads. Two sets of armour lay on the floor. It was the priest's impression that the men had killed themselves. By now, flames were roaring from the roof and burning calico was falling from the ceiling. Two policemen, Dwyer and Armstrong, had followed Gibney into the building. Between them, they were able to retrieve the body of Joe Byrne and carry out the wounded Martin Cherry but the bodies in the bedroom had to be left to the flames. One was starting to catch fire as they fled.

Crucially, Gibney later described the dead men in the bedroom as 'beardless boys'. The description clearly fit Dan and Steve. If these bodies were not those of the bushrangers then they must have been the mysterious swagmen. But none of the witness accounts mentioned these anonymous travellers. If the youthful and clean-shaven swaggies were there, then surely somebody would have seen fit to mention them later. It is hard to accept they even existed.

Constable Dwyer was the second man to see the bodies. A year later he told the Royal Commission he saw Dan Kelly's body with a wounded knee. (Dan had been shot in the leg during the final stages of the siege.) Dwyer said: 'I knew him to be Dan Kelly from the low forehead.' Asked if he could swear to Dan's identity, the policeman said: 'Yes, I knew the man with the black hair and sallow complexion was Dan Kelly.'

Supporters of the survival theory have questioned the validity of Dwyer's evidence, claiming he was unreliable and contradictory. This fits the belief that the police knew Dan and Steve were not dead and wanted it kept quiet. The Kelly outbreak had not reflected well on the police and the Royal Commission could shine light into some very dark corners. Dead bushrangers were better than live ones and this was an affair that needed to fade away. Dirty washing may well have been left unlaundered but in the case of the bodies in the bedroom, Dwyer's evidence dovetails with Gibney's, and the brave priest cannot be discredited.

The Kelly family provided more evidence that Dan and Steve died during the siege, the most powerful from Dan's mother. Reporter Brian Cookson stumbled on to journalistic gold when he toured Kelly Country in the very wet winter of 1910. He lost his way as he travelled through hills where pelting rain 'whistled mournful dirges' and the 'wetness came down in blinding sheets'. In a land awash, he sought shelter at a small cottage with a sliprail for the horses and a struggling garden. Here he was met by rosy-cheeked children and 'an ancient woman ... weighed down with some great, overpowering sorrow of the past'. The children were Ned Kelly's nieces and half-siblings. The ancient and sorrowful woman was his mother. Quite by accident, Cookson had stumbled across the home of Ellen Kelly and her brood of children and grandchildren.

As he dried out next to the fire, Cookson sympathetically asked Ellen about the rumours that Dan had survived.

'Dan is dead,' Ellen told the surprised reporter. 'No-one knows it better than I do.' And then in a voice that was almost a scream, she said:

If Dan Kelly was alive all these years wouldn't he have come to me? Would he let me want and go hungry, as I have done? Would he have seen me ending my life in this misery and done nothing to help me? Wouldn't he have told Jim?

Cookson had important evidence. A primary source—no less than Dan's mother—had no doubt her youngest son was dead these thirty years past. Well, she would say that, you might think. If Dan had lived, his mother would never give him up. But look at the words she chose. This was not a glib, oft-repeated denial but the heartfelt grief of a mother still mourning her lost sons: 'wouldn't he have come to me? . . . [Would he have] done nothing to help me?' Ellen's distraught words leave little doubt that she believed her son died at Glenrowan in 1880, and more importantly, Cookson believed her, too.

'They [Dan and Steve] are dead,' he reported. 'It is all very strange—and very sad as well.' It was strange and sad—and convincing, too. If Dan was alive then his mother did not know it, which is unthinkable for such a close family.

The Kelly family continued to deny that Dan had survived. In 1930, Jim Kelly wrote to the pro-Kelly author, JJ Kenneally: 'The name of my brother Dan has been used freely for sordid gain by a gang of impostors.' In 1922, Joseph Ashmead, a lifelong north-east resident and childhood friend of Dan Kelly wrote *The Briars and Thorns,* a rough personal account of the Kelly story. In it, Ashmead wrote there was 'not a shadow of doubt' that the bodies in the bedroom were those of Dan and Steve.

The repeated denials did little to dampen the survival story and Ellen's descendants, including her great-great-grandson

Anthony Griffiths, still speak out against it today. 'The family's got no doubts at all that they [Dan and Steve] perished at the siege,' Griffiths said in 2008.

> There's no doubt whatsoever and for that reason some of the claims that some of these characters went on to live in other areas and wanted nothing to do with their families were particularly hurtful because at that stage you have to remember that old Mrs [Ellen] Kelly was still alive and they were talking about one of her sons.

Noeleen Lloyd is also adamant that Dan and Steve died in the siege. She compares the survival theory to Elvis sightings and, like Anthony Griffiths, she hoped the absence of a cellar at the inn would kill off the story.

But mysterious old men with cloudy pasts had claimed to be the bushrangers, and some seemed to have a compelling case. If they were not Dan and Steve, then who were they, and what secrets did they hide? The best-known Dan Kelly claimant was James Ryan but the Ipswich vagrant's story is full of holes. Kelly family descendants say he was extensively questioned in the 1930s and he could not answer basic questions about the family's history. Apart from allegedly not even knowing the names of Ned's and Dan's sisters, he had a financial motive, as he had taken his tale to Sideshow Alley at the Brisbane Exhibition. And why would a man with a death penalty on his head announce to the world he was a wanted criminal? He could have proved his case at a time when Dan Kelly's family still lived, but he never did. Ryan's tale has intrigued some well-meaning people, but whoever he was, he was not Daniel Kelly.

Another Dan contender, Jack Day, died in 1943 and is buried on a station near Mount Isa. Also an anonymous bushman with no apparent past, Day was the right age and type of man to be Dan Kelly. He looked similar but apart from this strong physical resemblance to Dan and the suggestion that he sent money to Jim Kelly, there are no hard facts to show it is true. Without more than handed-down tales, the look-alike Jack Day can only be ruled out. The same goes for Billy Meade as Steve Hart. The only evidence that Meade was Steve came from Meade himself. Nobody will ever know why Billy confessed to being Steve but there is nothing to show he was telling the truth. The same must be said of Fred Layton. His claim is also based on physical similarities and folklore. Frederick Layton may have looked like Steve and Jack Day was the 'dead spit' of Dan Kelly but appearances can be deceiving. There are plenty of Elvis look-alikes but that does not make the king of rock 'n' roll any less dead.

Charles Tindall's claim is more credible, mainly because he tried to keep it secret. There was something in his past he kept hidden all his long life and it is tempting to imagine he had some connection with the Kelly Gang. Perhaps he might even have been at the siege, possibly as a sympathiser. Like James Ryan, Charles had suffered serious burns at some time in his past life. There was no obvious reason for Tindall to lie and he never sought to make money from his story. He wanted no-one to know except his nearest and dearest.

Charles Devine Tindall had a secret. At some time between the burning of the inn and the Great War, he became a different man. It might have been the danger of being part of the Kellys that led him to a new life, or his secret might be more human and mundane. But again, there is only his word and an intriguing scribble in a prayer book to back up his claim to being Dan Kelly. It is not enough to overcome the solid evidence that Dan and Steve died at the inn. So who was he really? Sadly for his granddaughter Maureen Tyler, we'll probably never know. But he cannot have been Dan Kelly.

Finally, there is the cellar. If there was a cellar beneath the kitchen, why did Ann Jones not put her children there when the shooting started? Men were sheltering behind chaff bags in the kitchen but surely a bolthole below the ground would have been a better place to take cover. And even if the cellar does exist, would it have been enough to protect two men from a fire so intense that it melted glass into aerated bubbles? The tragic deaths of seven people in backyard fire bunkers during Victoria's Black Saturday bushfires in February 2009 indicates that it would not.

In a report on the dig released in 2010, Adam Ford briefly addressed the Dan and Steve survival theory. The report says that the dig could not provide evidence either way except to confirm there was no cellar under the inn, and that if there is a cellar under the residence it still will not prove the story is true. Ford's report noted the survival theory is supported by only a minority of Kelly enthusiasts. Tiny fragments of bone were recovered from the rear bedroom, however, and it was hoped they might have been the incinerated remains of the two men found dead there. If so, the fragments might have provided evidence about their deaths, and might even be proved to belong to Dan and Steve. Testing later found most of the bone fragments were too small to identify and the largest was from an animal. Adam Ford's report concluded that even if the smaller bones were human 'it will not categorically prove that Dan and Steve died during the siege but will reinforce the eyewitness accounts'.

Gary Dean and others still hope to excavate the kitchen and residence so the cellar story can be proved or disproved. Dean thinks it is likely that a cellar is there and that it might contain evidence to show that two men could have hidden there in 1880. Perhaps the residence will be excavated one day and the question of the cellar will be answered. DNA testing of descendants and claimants might yet yield some information, but the survival theory will probably live on regardless. Like Elvis, Dan and Steve will never really die.

As in many country graveyards, the headstones in the Greta cemetery carry the names of families who can trace their roots back to settlement but at Greta it is the missing headstones that best explain the community as it was in the Kelly years. Ned's sister Maggie Skillian was buried there without a headstone in 1896. Ellen Kelly lies there too. She died in 1923, poor all her life but dignified and respected in her later years. Her grave is also unmarked, as is that of her son Jim, who was buried there in 1946.

Dan Kelly and Steve Hart are almost certainly there, too. There were reports that Steve was buried under a fig tree near Wangaratta and Dan on the banks of the Eleven Mile Creek but it is widely accepted that both were laid to rest in unmarked graves at the Greta cemetery, hours after a riotous wake. While it is true the police had released the bodies to the families almost immediately after the siege, it does not prove anybody was trying to hide their identities. Rather, it was probably a prudent piece of policing. Hundreds of furious family members and sympathisers were gathered in Glenrowan as the siege ended and the police feared a bloodbath if the bodies were not handed over. There was no more to it than that. Dan and Steve were buried the next day and the ground over their graves might have been ploughed to hide the traces. If anybody knows exactly where the bodies lie, then they are not saying. But it can be said with certainty that Dan Kelly and Steve Hart died at Ann Jones' inn on 28 June 1880. Unless startling new evidence emerges, they should be left to rest in peace.

12
THE HOUSE OF SPORT

'But sure Ned was a darling man.'

It was cold outside and the fires were blazing in the parlour and dining room. Most of the men were still at the inn while the women and children remained at the stationmaster's home where Steve Hart was keeping an eye on them. At the hotel, Thomas Curnow joined Dan Kelly. Joe Byrne walked by and glanced at Dan's glass. 'Be careful, old man,' warned Joe. 'All right,' said Dan, and he added some water to his brandy. Joe would have done better to follow his own advice; in just a few hours he would raise a stiff drink in his last living act.

Some eighteen hours had passed since the shooting of Aaron Sherritt and there was still no sign of the police train. The hostages were getting restless, and restless prisoners could mean escaped prisoners. Entertainment was in order. Ann's good table was removed from the dining room to the verandah and a 'dance was got up'. Ann and Jane were the only women there so they danced with Steve and Dan and the rest of the men danced with each other while David Mortimer played Johnny

Jones' concertina. Ann later noted that Ned was not much of a dancer, although he made a very fine host, albeit one with two revolvers.

THE DANCE AT THE GLENROWAN INN BEFORE THE FIGHT.

The dance at the Glenrowan Inn before the fight, wood engraving by Mr T Carrington, published 17 July 1880. Image courtesy of the Pictures Collection, State Library of Victoria.

Ann knew that she was in the company of dangerous men and a wrong move could be deadly—but on the other hand if she played her cards right, she might be well placed for the future. So, now that the Kellys were here (at her invitation) perhaps this shocking upheaval could be turned to her advantage. A little flattery might work. After all, they were only men. Loudly she praised Ned: 'What a fine fellow he is!' she exclaimed. She would be pleased if the gang stayed a week!

Perhaps, at the time, she even meant it. In any case, it could not do any harm to befriend the gang and if the power base really was shifting then she was in a good position. If not, then who could blame her for going through the motions of submitting to armed and desperate outlaws with murder on their minds? Besides, it was shaping up to be a busy afternoon at the inn and she expected everybody to pay for their drinks.

It was also quite a thrill. Glenrowan had never seen such excitement and nor would it again. The Kellys had burst into town in such an explosion of drama that it was easy to forget how volatile this situation really was. Life in a bush town in 1880 could be marked by drudgery and hard labour. But now there was an air of celebration and some of the prisoners were starting to enjoy themselves. In Ann's words, the Glenrowan Inn was becoming a 'House of Sport'. In sport, though, there are always winners and losers, and Thomas Curnow was forming a plan to put the Kelly Gang on the losing side.

The schoolmaster had been standing in the rear yard thinking about the plans to wreck the train. He 'keenly felt that it was my duty to do anything that I could to prevent the outrage which the outlaws had planned'. It was then that Dan Kelly invited Thomas to join the dancing. In a drawing by the artist Thomas Carrington, Ned presides over the dancing in his armour and oilskin coat. The drawing is rather misleading, as all four sets of armour were locked away in the eastern bedroom at this time, but the drawing does show the men enjoying a good old-fashioned country 'knees-up' and gives a lively impression of how the hostage-taking turned into a party.

Thomas asked Ned to accompany him home to fetch his dancing shoes but Ned refused because they would have to pass the police barracks to get to the Curnow home, so Thomas had to make do with his boots. One boot had a thick sole to compensate for his hip deformity and it was difficult for him to dance gracefully but he gamely did his best, all the while secretly pondering how to save the train. Like Ann, Thomas soon came to the conclusion that he would have to win the gang's trust so he started to flatter Ned and hinted that he was a fervent sympathiser. Always keen to believe people were on his side, Ned began to be taken in.

Soon the entertainment moved outdoors, where Ned organised some sporting contests. There were feats on horseback and Ned joined in a game of hop, step and jump—still with a revolver in each hand. At about this time, Thomas was allowed to walk the short distance to the stationmaster's home to check on his family. It was there that Thomas noticed his sister's red scarf. He thought, 'What a splendid danger signal it would make,' and he became even more anxious to escape. The scarf that kept Catherine Curnow warm on that cold day would soon become part of Australian folklore.

Thomas quickly found further opportunities to ingratiate himself with the gang. First he tended to Steve's sore feet and then Dan Kelly arrived at the Stanistreets' home looking for a small bag he had misplaced. Thomas did not know what the parcel contained but Dan 'seemed very anxious about it' and Thomas made a show of searching the house. 'They thanked me, and I perceived that I had in a great measure obtained their confidence by telling me this.' Later, he sidled up to Ned and confided that John Stanistreet kept a revolver in his home. Stanistreet would not use the gun against the gang, Thomas said, but somebody else might. Ned thanked the schoolmaster and confiscated the gun. Thomas Curnow's deception of Ned Kelly was almost complete.

At about this time, Ned heard that a circus was travelling through the region and he briefly considered bailing up the troupe as it passed by on the Melbourne to Sydney road. They could have provided professional amusement for the gang and prisoners but Ned let the entertainers continue on their way past the inn, and out of history. Ned already had too many hostages and another group, no matter how entertaining, would be too hard to handle.

Late in the afternoon, Ned ordered the women and children to be brought over to the inn. The arrival of the women sparked up the party and there was more dancing inside while a bonfire roared in the rear yard. The number of hostages reached its peak, with more than sixty people crammed into and around the building. Ann spent some time playing cards with Ned in the parlour. She never said what they talked about but, in her mood to flatter, she may well have complimented the handsome bushranger on his clothes. Ned was a snappy dresser. For his final night of freedom, he wore a flamboyant 'larrikin' outfit of strapped trousers, high-heeled boots and a striking polka-dotted shirt. Around his waist was the green sash that he had been awarded for saving the life of the boy Richard Shelton some fifteen years earlier.

It says much about Ned that he wore the sash for the moment that he knew would define him. Somehow, through years of imprisonment and months on the run, he had managed to keep it. More than an eye-catching addition to his wardrobe, it was tangible proof of the 'good' Ned, the Ned Kelly who could lay undiluted claim to decency and honour. He had spent the last two years of his life trying to make people believe that he was a good man made bad by provocation and injustice. The two-metre sash around his waist was testament to how Ned saw himself and how he wanted others to see him, too.

Thanks to Ned Kelly, Richard Shelton survived until old age and had twelve children. He would never say much about Ned Kelly in later years, except 'he was all right'. Richard Shelton's grandson, Bill Shelton, who lives at Avenel, agrees.

> We feel that Ned was fairly harshly done by. The Kellys were certainly a downtrodden family and the 'wallopers' gave them a pretty tough time. You can get sick of that.

Ned had no way of knowing that the farce at the Sherritt hut had fatally delayed his plan. In Benalla, Superintendent Hare received the telegram reporting Aaron's murder at about half past two that afternoon. He had men and horses as well as two Aboriginal troopers and could have struck at the gang immediately. For some reason that he never explained, Hare instead chose to wait until he could order in some reinforcements. By the time Hare was able to contact Commissioner Standish in Melbourne it was half past four. Then several more hours were lost while a special train was organised and men and horses assembled. The train would not leave Melbourne until ten pm, more than twenty-four hours after the murder of Aaron Sherritt.

Meanwhile, the news quickly spread to other ears, including those of Thomas Carrington, the reporter and artist with the *Australasian Sketcher*. Carrington was on his way to share 'a glass of grog' with a friend in Melbourne when he decided to stop at the office. It was lucky for him that he did for there he found a telegram with the 'startling intelligence that the Kellys had broken out again and shot a man'. Carrington hastened to Spencer Street station but if he had hoped for an exclusive he was disappointed because when he arrived he found other reporters already there. They would join the police train and get the story of the century.

Late in the evening, Ned announced his intention of taking Bracken into custody. It was strange that the policeman had been left alone for so long. Perhaps Ned thought Bracken's illness meant he was not a threat. In any case, Thomas Curnow saw it as the chance he had been waiting for. The Curnow home lay beyond the police barracks and Thomas asked if he and his family would be permitted to go home when Ned picked up Bracken. Thomas assured Ned 'he had no case for fearing me as I was with him heart and soul'. Ned replied, 'I know that, and I can see it', and with that he agreed to allow Thomas and his family to accompany him to the barracks. It was a serious mistake.

Another hour or two passed before Ned finally prepared to leave. At last, he and Joe retrieved their armour from the bedroom and buckled it on. Now, with the Curnow family trotting alongside in their gig, they set off in the dark and frosty night to take the last of the Glenrowaners hostage.

Hugh Bracken was one of the 'good guys' in the police—even Kelly supporters had noted he was decent and honest. The goodwill between Ned and Bracken had been longstanding. Soon after Ned was released from Beechworth Gaol for the first time, nine years earlier, Bracken had visited the Kelly home at Greta to try to persuade the boys to go straight. Obviously, the policeman's good advice was not heeded but Ned must have been impressed. He later said of Bracken: 'There's a man I wouldn't have the heart to shoot.'

Equally, Bracken was determined to do his duty to catch the Kellys. He had even at one time worked for the police for no pay so he could join the search for the gang but he never expected to be bailed up in his own home by Ned Kelly himself. When Ned entered the Bracken home at about half past eleven on the night of the twenty-seventh, the policeman at first thought it was a joke, a prank to 'try my pluck'. But when the tall intruder wearing what appeared to be 'a nail can' on his head announced, 'I'm Ned Kelly, put up your hands,' Hugh Bracken realised the matter was deadly serious. Perhaps mindful of the trauma he had inflicted on the Bracken family Ned took the hand of the policeman's young son as he left the house, and said: 'I may be worth £2000 to you yet, my child.'

After Bracken was safely under guard, Thomas, his wife and his sister were allowed to go home. They set out through the darkness, Ned's final words ringing in the teacher's ears: 'Go quietly to bed, and don't dream too loud!' The schoolmaster had no doubt about the threat implied in the seemingly friendly words. Ned took Bracken back to the inn and Thomas prepared for an act that would change his life. The train was now steaming steadily northwards to Glenrowan.

When Ned and Joe returned to the hotel with their prisoner, the party was in full swing. Joe locked the front door and casually placed the key on a mantelpiece. Dan Kelly, who apparently did not share Ned's high opinion of Bracken, suggested the policeman should be shot, or at least handcuffed. Ned refused, saying Bracken should 'be left as he is'. Bracken, meanwhile, took note of the key on the mantelpiece and when no-one was looking, he quietly slipped it into his trousers. Although unwell, the brave policeman was continuing to do his duty.

Drinks were being served at the bar, people were dancing and feet tapped along in time to David Mortimer on the concertina. Ned called for a song and frail Johnny Jones was put forward. The song that Johnny chose was 'The Wild Colonial Boy'—the ballad of the teenage bushranger Jack Doolan.

> There was a wild colonial boy,
> Jack Doolan was his name
> Of poor but honest parents,
> He was born in Castlemaine

The irony of the rollicking tale could not have been lost on Ned as the crowd stamped on the wooden floor and sang along. The rooms must have shaken as the chorus rang out . . .

> So come away, me hearties
> We'll roam the mountains high
> Together we will plunder
> And together we will die

The party reached a high note as the rebellious story of Jack Doolan raised the roof of Ann's fine inn. And when young Jack Doolan fought his gunbattle with the three troopers, did Ned spare a thought for Kennedy, Lonigan and Scanlan?

> Jack drew his pistol from his belt
> And waved it like a toy,

'I'll fight, but not surrender,' cried
The wild colonial boy

And when the Wild Colonial Boy fell with shattered jaws, still fighting as his life ran out, did Ned think for a moment that life was about to imitate art? Perhaps he was caught up in the foot-stamping cry of defiance, and perhaps he still thought his rebellion would end in glory. Or, maybe, he secretly knew that he, too, would soon meet a similar dreadful fate.

And that's the way they captured him,
The wild colonial boy

Young Johnny Jones was then called upon to sing one more song, 'Cailín Deas Crúite na mBó', or 'A Pretty Girl Milking Her Cow'. This was a popular nineteenth-century ballad, originally sung in Gaelic. It tells of a young man smitten by the sight of a beautiful milkmaid with cheeks 'redder than the rowan trees'. The love-struck young man cannot bear the thought of life without her. Curiously poignant, the old folk song must have changed the defiant mood in the pub and we can imagine young Johnny's high, clear voice silencing the inn as this most Irish of songs faded at the end.

It was a clear, cold night with a bright moon and the Southern Cross hung low in the sky at the front of the inn. Outdoors, breath steamed in soft, grey plumes. There would be a fog or mist in the morning. The bonfire roared in the rear yard, while inside the fires in both hearths were so high that Ann feared her mantelpieces would catch alight. She was also concerned that some of the Glenrowaners were not paying for their brandy, rum or wine. This, of course, would prove to be the least of her problems.

The outlaws had had their fill of Ann's liquor. Steve Hart had knocked off 'six noggins of brandy' that morning and, according to Hanorah McDonnell, Steve feared that if he 'took another he might lose his head'. But Steve sobered up as the day progressed and managed to fulfil his task of guarding the women and children at the Stanistreets' home.

Joe Byrne was a man who liked to celebrate and he had been drinking, too. Apart from his fondness for a drink, he was also an opium user. He was close to the Chinese community and could speak some Cantonese. He obtained the opium from the Chinese miners and it was well known that he often smoked it with them. Although there is no indication he was using opium during or before the siege, he started drinking soon after arriving in Glenrowan and this might have contributed to the mistakes made by the gang. Joe's need for a drink was perhaps not surprising; the brandies may well have helped to lay some ghosts to rest. After all, it had been less than twenty-four hours since he had murdered a lifelong friend in front of two distraught women.

As the party continued, Ned and Ann spent some time outside in the starry night. Witnesses told of an incident between the two—'a moment against the fence'. The full nature of the 'moment' might never be known but several people saw Ann with her arm around the bushranger's neck and there were later newspaper reports that she had boasted of kissing him. Ann later denied any physical intimacy between the two but there is no doubt that, at the least, she did have an arm around the charismatic bushranger. It was a strange development between two people who distrusted each other. Earlier that day, Ned said he 'had a mind to blow a hole in that woman' but now they seemed to be close. Ann later wrote a letter that reveals much about the dynamics between the men and women in the House of Sport.

> . . . the people did not think about the special [train] it took up their attention watching the gang as they were noble looking men . . . the divil was in us we had . . . to be looking at the darling men but sure Ned was a darling man.

Perhaps it was just a sham, a desperate ploy to protect her children and her home. Or maybe, like Mrs Scott of Euroa and Mrs Devine of Jerilderie, the lady of the house at Glenrowan was falling under the spell of Ned Kelly. Whatever her motives, these actions would come back to haunt her. For his part, Ned must have been lonely and maybe a little frightened. He was exceptionally close to his imprisoned mother, Ellen, and maybe he drew comfort from Ann, who had more in common with Ellen than either woman would have admitted.

It was a thrilling time, too, for Ann's daughter Jane. She looked older than her fourteen years and was nearing marriageable age but she was still an impressionable country girl who had never seen such goings-on. In an interview with *The Ovens and Murray Advertiser* after the siege, Jane said:

> Three rooms were full of the people who had been bailed up. Both front and back doors were left open, and as no-one was keeping guard any one could have got away.

Jane neglected to mention that she had helped to make sure that the prisoners in fact could not get away. She had been using a revolver as a pointer to count heads among the crowd and had threatened to tell Ned if anybody discussed escaping. Jane, meanwhile, had fallen for the charms of Steve Hart. Earlier, Steve had laid his head in Jane's lap (Steve had told her he was ill) and now they were dancing together. Her former classmate, the teenage hostage Tom Cameron, was not impressed. Tom wrote to his brother: 'Jenny Jones was making free with [Dan and Steve], getting on their knees and dancing with them and kissing them. I think six months in gaol would do her no harm.'

Clearly, young Thomas took a hard line on law and order. Or maybe he was just jealous. It must have been a dangerously exciting time for young Jane but her fun would be short-lived. Soon she would be wounded by a police bullet and within two years she would be dead.

In Melbourne, the special train was warming up at Spencer Street station. Finally, with a hiss of steam, it chuffed away from the platform just a few minutes before ten pm. There was one locomotive, one carriage and a brake van. On board were a party of police, five crew and the journalists George Allen for *The Daily Telegraph*, Joe Melvin of *The Argus* and John McWhirter for *The Age*, as well as Carrington of the *Sketcher*. The train stopped at Essendon and collected the police inspector Stanhope O'Connor and his team of five Aboriginal troopers from Queensland. These men were greatly feared by Ned Kelly, who loathed them for their uncanny ability to track fugitives through the wilderness. He had described them as 'little black devils' and saw them as such a danger that he later made special mention of his intention to kill them in the train crash.

Also at Essendon, two unexpected passengers boarded the train. Ned Kelly might have been taken aback to know that Sub-Inspector O'Connor's wife and her sister had decided at the last minute to join the journey. The ladies thought it an exciting adventure and a chance to see the gold rush town of Beechworth. Luckily, there was a first-class carriage for them.

McWhirter later reported in *The Age* that the train travelled at great speed (a dizzying 64 kilometres an hour) after leaving Essendon and despite being damaged when it crashed through a gate near Craigieburn, it reached Benalla at about half past one on the morning of the twenty-eighth. There it collected Francis Hare, another eight police, two more Aboriginal troopers and a number of horses. At about this time, word may have reached the police that the Kellys had tampered with the rail line. After some discussion and another short delay, it was decided to send a pilot engine ahead as lookout. At about two o'clock on that clear, moonlit but bitterly cold morning, both engines started the final leg of the journey to Glenrowan. There were now twenty-four people on board the police special.

Thomas Curnow and his family reached home within minutes of leaving the police barracks. Thomas quietly gathered a candle, some matches and his sister's red scarf. He could only assume the train was making its way north so he intended to ride as close to the railway line as he could, hoping to reach Benalla before the train left. But his wife, Jean, became hysterical when she learned her husband intended to stop the train. She feared she, her sister-in-law and her baby would be murdered so Thomas took his family to Jean's mother's house at a nearby farm. He hoped she would stay with her mother while he completed his dangerous mission 'but Mrs Curnow was exceedingly anxious to get home again and would not stay there'. Thomas then took his wife home again, where he told his last lie—that he had given up his plan to stop the train. Satisfied, Jean went to bed and Thomas was free to leave.

He set out on foot in the dark, fearing a bullet in the back at any minute. He was almost too late; within moments he heard the chugging of the train in the frozen air. Thomas lit his candle and held it up behind his sister's scarf. Just a little over a mile out of Glenrowan, the guard on the pilot engine saw a tiny red glow in the darkness. The pilot loco stopped and Thomas Curnow called out: 'It's the Kellys!'

As the train prepared to leave Benalla, the party at Ann Jones' inn was winding down. The people were tired and some were doubtless the worse for drink. Ned had already released some twenty trusted 'hostages', including the McDonnells, but there were still about forty people at the inn. At around two o'clock, Ned finally decided the train would not come and everybody could go. They started to file out the front door into the frosty night. And then Ann, perhaps flushed with excitement or keen to leave a positive impression on the dashing bushrangers, made a decision that would blight her life. Although she later denied it, several witnesses said she called the hostages back inside. She then uttered some fateful words.

'You are not to go yet,' she announced. 'Kelly is to give you a lecture.'

The hostages turned away from the night and back into the warm pub. As the minutes ticked by on Ann's wall clock, Ned took centre stage and delivered his lecture. The people at the inn should by now have been on their way home, safe with memories of a remarkable night to amaze their grandchildren. Instead, they listened as Ned verbally jousted with some of his prisoners. He advised James Reardon against 'being too fond of getting out of bed till you are called out of it' and in what seems to have been a moment of high rhetoric, he asked the rail-way man Sullivan if he was 'Sullivan the murderer'—a loathed informer whom Ned would 'give a thousand pounds for'. With another threat to shoot anybody who aided the police against him, Ned concluded his lecture in a jocular exchange with Bracken. At last, after about half an hour, with laughter echoing around the pub, the speech was over and the hostages were free to go.

And then Joe Byrne burst into the bar from the passageway. 'The train is coming!' he cried.

The gang rushed into the bedroom to collect their armour. The siege of the Glenrowan Inn was about to begin.

13
BURIED TREASURES

'It made that moment real to me.'

The setbacks and delays had proved costly but by the start of the third week, the archaeologists could say their major structural goals had been reached. The inn had been found and there was tangible evidence of the gunfight, seen in the molten scraps of spent bullets. It meant the project had met its scientific and historical targets and now the diggers were right on top of the occupation layer they were looking for—Ann Jones' inn. It was hoped the site was about to yield some very human evidence about the life and death of the pub. To get there, the team had had to go through layers of the twentieth century first and there was a mountain of items that needed to be processed. They had to be stored somewhere and luckily the place to do it was just up the road.

In 1888, the government built a new police station and residence in Glenrowan. It was a solid six-roomed brick house east of the inn on Siege Street. The town's police—usually a sole officer accompanied by his family—lived and worked there for more than a century until the town's third police station was built on the other side of the railway line. The old station is now used as a community hall. During the dig, it was taken over by the archaeologists as a headquarters and 'incident room' for the artefacts from the dig.

Ironically, the police had occupied the site of Ann Jones' inn for several years in the 1880s. Five months after the siege, Ann was charged with harbouring the outlaws and, although she was acquitted at trial, the damage had been done to her reputation. She built a new hotel on the ashes of the first one but the authorities felt she was not a 'fit and proper person' and they refused to grant her a liquor licence. By 1884 she had little choice but to lease out the new building—and it was the police who became the tenants. They moved into Ann's second hotel until the new station was built four years later. The police must have been delighted at the symbolism of occupying the very place where the Kellys had held them at bay.

During the dig, thousands of items collected from the site were stored in plastic baskets throughout the cold, high-ceilinged rooms of the old police house. The police family's former living room was converted into a conservator's station with a large desk, strong lights and a microscope. Finds that were more promising, or deemed to be at risk of deterioration, were brought to the desk, where they were patiently cleaned and treated. Less valuable material was stored elsewhere in the house, eventually cascading out on to the concrete verandah, where stacks of baskets carried odds and ends gleaned from the narrow block.

On television, archaeology moves at a cracking pace. The reality is far less exciting. Apart from the hard labour of shifting great quantities of soil by hand, someone has to clean, sort and process the bits and pieces that come out of it. This less-than-glamorous job went to volunteers and students who cheerily cleaned their way through the mountain of items that, at first glance, seemed to be nothing but junk. Actually, most of it was junk. Among a handful of valuable items were chunks of roof tile, broken bricks, coils of wire, rusted nuts and bolts and countless shards of glass and pottery. It was scrubbed, classified into baskets and recorded—each item a tiny footnote added to the site's history. A few important artefacts were kept aside and, for the last time, the rest of it was thrown away.

The amount of useless rubbish recovered began to fall as the dig progressed. As expected, construction, demolition and agriculture over the years had scrambled some of the remnants of the original inn into the upper layers and many of these were found early in the dig. The finds included balls of molten glass that must once have been deemed so worthless they had even escaped the predations of souvenir hunters. It was a good thing they had because they helped to solve the problem of how to interpret the two fires on the site.

The glass pieces were very smooth with rounded edges and inside they were shot with bubbles of oxygen. It was evidence of melting at extreme temperatures, probably with the help of an accelerant. It seemed the ten gallons of flammable spirits that Ann had lost in the fire had helped to cause the intensity of the inferno that destroyed the inn. By contrast, the second fire must have been much cooler and had left very little trace. The signs were good that high-quality material would soon be found.

One of the most important finds came midway through the third week when a large coin was found beneath a layer of ash in the dining room area. It lay under the line of the window where the front wall would have met the verandah. When it was cleaned, it proved to be a penny minted in 1876. Significantly, its location beneath the ash layer indicated that it was deposited there prior to or even during the siege. It was the first definitive dating evidence found at the site. Also, the coin had not been affected by heat, which meant it was below the floorboards when the inn caught fire. It could be said with certainty that it had been lost some time between the construction of the inn in 1878 and its fiery end two years later. We will never know who lost the coin, or how, but it is easy to imagine it might have fallen from a pocket during the party on the eve of the battle. If so, it would have rolled through the dining room floorboards and onto the earth, where it lay undisturbed for at least 128 years.

Of a total of 11,180 items ultimately drawn from the ground and processed in the gloomy old police station, 501 could be definitely linked to Ann's occupation of the site. Most were everyday items—broken pots, lost buttons, pieces of molten window glass or rusted nails. But when they were pieced together, they began to tell a story about the people who lived there, and in particular, how the rooms were furnished.

A small rod that could have been mistaken for a twig was cleaned up and found to have been a slate pencil. Fifteen fragments of a ruled slate writing board were found in the same area. An artefact report later noted that slates were cheap and common writing implements in the late nineteenth century. They were usually associated with the education of children, so it is possible Ann's children might have used the slate pencils for their homework, set by the teacher, Mr Curnow. As the slate pieces were found near the bar, however, it is also possible they were used for business, perhaps to write food orders or keep accounts. This could explain the fragmentation of the slate board. Witnesses later told of clocks and other fittings being shattered in the gunfight. If the board had been hanging above the bar, then it is fair to assume it, too, would have been blasted to pieces by police bullets.

Post holes sometimes act as traps for artefacts because as the timber decays it leaves a void and small items can find their way into the space, either naturally or by backfilling in later construction phases. The post holes from the front rooms were especially productive, including one from the parlour area. This was associated with a later building, most probably Ann's second hotel. When the hole had been dug and the post inserted, loose soil from the edges was packed in and tamped down. This soil contained fragments of the battle, including a molten bullet from a police pistol. It was a rich little post hole; there was also a lump of molten glass fused with an iron nail and a silver sixpence from 1859.

It was a post hole from the bar that yielded one of the project's most poignant finds—a small but heavy glass sphere crusted in dirt. When the dirt was washed off, it proved to be a pitted but intact 'swirl' marble made in Germany between 1846 and 1880. Because it was found beneath a post hole from the original inn, the blue and white marble could be linked to the short life of the first building and therefore the family of Ann Jones. It seemed likely the marble was lost by one of Ann Jones' four boys between 1878 and 1880. It was the only toy associated with the Jones children found on the site and it served as a solitary reminder that five of Ann's children endured the siege and one did not survive.

Dozens of nondescript ceramic and glass shards were collected and put away for analysis. Some of the shards came from Ann Jones' inn and they later provided an insight into the way she ran her hotel and how she wanted to be perceived. On their own they seemed no more than useless scraps but patient reconstruction later drew the pieces together to draw a detailed picture of how Ann would have set her table. It was established that most of the plates and vessels Ann used were made in Staffordshire, England. This was quite telling. Australian potteries had been established by Ann's time but they mostly made utilitarian goods. The Staffordshire products, on the other hand, were produced with an American market in mind and were of relatively high quality. The discoveries showed that Ann served food on white 25- and 28-centimetre plates; her guests were offered soup in tureens; and tea was enjoyed in gilt-banded cups.

Other tiny fragments provided a further illustration of the feminine influence Ann brought to the pub's decor. These shards also appeared meaningless when they came out of the ground but they were later found to be parts of a flowerpot, a mirror, a figurine and decorative glass. Blasted apart by bullets or scorched by fire, these forgotten remnants of the inn proved that while the pub might have been a rough bush shanty from the outside, there was a relatively refined and tasteful look inside. There might also have been mugs and utensils made of pewter, as Ann had listed these goods as being lost in the fire, but no pewter was recovered. It is likely the melted remains of these items were taken by souvenir hunters.

Ann's boast of 'Best Accommodation' on the sign outside the pub was borne out by the ceramics she provided for her guests. They included 'a set of floral green transfer-printed toiletware vessels, including a ewer, dish and a matching red-banded chamber pot', dated post 1828. The artefact report noted that they would have formed a matched set used in a bedroom. When Ann's guests needed to relieve themselves they had a tastefully decorated chamber pot in which to do it. There were plenty of melted glass and bottle fragments, too. After all, this *was* a pub. The remains of three clay pipestems showed some of Ann's guests enjoyed a smoke with their drinks or after their meal. The pipe fragments were particularly poignant to the hostage descendant Judith Douthie, who came to Glenrowan hoping for a closer contact with Ann Jones but instead found an unexpected connection with a broken pipestem.

> Tom Cameron talked about how Ned frightened the living daylights out of John Delaney, and it was Tom who'd lent a pipe to John to have a smoke with, and he crushed the pipe to pieces in fright. Even though it didn't happen at the inn, the sight of the pipe stem made that moment real to me.

The shattered remains of Ann's fine glassware and ceramics also revealed much about the contents of her bar. We now know that her guests would have drunk from ceramic mugs made in Germany or sipped schnapps from Holland. Beer was served in an amber bottle, gin from a clear, square one. Non-drinkers could order aerated water from a bottle sealed with a marble stopper. And if they were ill, the gin and schnapps might be a tonic. In fact, these spirits were often used for medicinal purposes so they could also be classified among the pharmaceutical finds. Among those were at least four medicine bottles, including a whiteware ointment jar that offered 'infallible cure for all diseases of the eye'. This amazing product was probably in use during Ann's second occupation of the site.

The Chinese influence on the times also became evident when most of the base and lid from a Chinese pot were reassembled from more than a dozen scraps. There was evidence of the first Australians, too; a stone cutting tool was a reminder that Aboriginal people lived on or near the site for tens of thousands of years. But the artefact report noted that in this most Irish of stories, with an Irish publican and an Irish outlaw gang, none of the items found on the site were produced in the old country.

These pieces of Ann Jones' life were excavated mostly without comment, and before they were analysed it was difficult to establish their worth. There had been more than enough finds already, however, for the archaeologists to know they had reached at least part of their target. Importantly, the inn had been found and plotted and the team could now say with certainty that its remains not only still existed but were now recorded for posterity.

On the other hand, there was a lingering sense of disappointment at being unable to excavate Ann's kitchen and home. This part of the job had always been subject to budget and time constraints and the priority had to be a complete and thorough excavation of the inn. It is likely the Jones' home would have yielded more personal touches than the hotel had and it also offered the tantalising possibility of a conclusive answer on the existence of a cellar. Whatever still lies under Ann's home will remain there indefinitely and it was frustrating to have to leave those questions unanswered.

There were many remnants of the inn and its furnishings—more than expected—and the recovery of such a large number of police bullets fired into the building was a welcome surprise. In fact, remnants of the bullets fired by the police kept coming up, right through the final days of the dig. These were important finds, adding to the growing list of artefacts that could be linked to the police attack or the contents of the inn. With three days to go, the dig could be classed as a success in scientific and historical terms—but, from the layperson's perspective, just a little something was missing. That missing ingredient was the Kellys themselves.

14
THE BATTLE

'You can't hurt me! I'm in iron!'

A metallic clanking rang through the pub as the sympathiser James Kershaw helped the gang put on their heavy suits of armour. Kershaw, the son of a convict, was there as a willing 'hostage' but he took no part in the gunfight that was about to erupt. Now wearing his armour, Ned slipped out the back door and mounted his horse. He silently rode along the railway line and saw the train halted at a cutting about 2 kilometres short of the station. He hurried back to the inn where he ordered Ann to extinguish the fires and the lamps. Steam hissed angrily in the fireplaces. Mothers drew their children close as the window blinds were drawn and darkness closed over the inn. From the outside, it appeared deserted.

Ned crept back down to the rail line. The pilot engine and train had now been coupled together and were crawling towards the station. It was obvious the police had been warned about the damage to the tracks but if Ned still hoped the train would keep going he was to be disappointed. Belching steam, it eased to a halt at the station. There was a clatter as the police began to unload their horses and Ned had to make a decision. There was still time for the gang to slip away in the darkness. They could melt into the hills and rally for another try. But the sympathisers had already gathered and a plan was irrevocably in place. It was too late to go back. Ned decided to bring things to a head. He crept through the darkness to rejoin his men at the inn.

What he did not know was that Hugh Bracken had plans of his own. While Ned was gone, Bracken had quietly moved around the inn, instructing the hostages to lie on the floor or seek cover where they could, probably saving many lives. Then when the prisoners were as safe as they could be, and the rest of the gang was distracted, he used the key he had pocketed earlier and slipped out the front door.

Superintendent Hare was supervising the unloading at the station when Bracken dashed up in the bright moonlight. The artist Thomas Carrington was standing near Hare. Carrington reported that Bracken gasped out: 'Over there—the Kellys ... the four of them—quick, quick!' Bracken then galloped off to Wangaratta to fetch reinforcements. There is no evidence that Bracken told Hare the inn was also full of hostages, but then Hare did not ask. In this battle, the police would shoot first and ask questions later.

Hare rallied his men and bravely rushed towards the hotel. It was a sudden and ill-considered assault but he must have seen it as the moment to capture the gang in one rapid blow and end two years of torment. With his men in tow, Hare raced across the railway reserve towards the inn. There was a fence with an iron pedestrian gate between the station and the inn and when Hare rushed the gate he became the first casualty of the battle.

Bird's eye view of Glenrowan, wood engraving published 17 July 1880.
Image courtesy of the Pictures Collection, State Library of Victoria.

The full moon shone brightly over Morgan's Lookout behind the inn, casting a deep shadow along the verandah. The outlaws had fanned out in the darkness and as Hare charged the gate Ned took aim, peering through the narrow slit of his helmet and steadying his revolving rifle. Hare had been hunting the Kellys since the Stringybark Creek killings and now it was the moment of reckoning. Ned pulled the trigger at a distance of less than 20 metres and the first shot rang out in the frosty air. The bullet smashed into Hare's left arm. 'Good gracious! I am hit!' he cried, as blood sprayed from his shattered wrist. It was the first blood shed at the Glenrowan siege.

Thomas Carrington, who was observing from the relative safety of the railway station, reported that the first shot was 'instantly followed by a dozen others, until the whole of the front of the house seemed in a blaze of light'. All four members of the Kelly Gang were firing rapidly from the darkness in front of the inn and the roar of rifles and crack of striking bullets was chaotic. Carrington said the bullets 'came whistling and pinging about us'. One hit the train and another flew across the railway line and smashed into the mantelpiece at McDonnell's Hotel. Carrington wrote:

The first brush was exceedingly hot. The police and the gang blazed away at each other in the darkness furiously. It lasted for about a quarter of an hour, and during that time there was nothing but a succession of flashes and reports, the pinging of bullets in the air, and the shrieks of women who had been made prisoners in the hotel.

The police ducked for cover behind trees and in ditches and poured fire at the inn. Hare staggered back to the station where Carrington dressed his wound. The policeman did not realise how badly he had been injured. He was feeling little pain but the bone was broken and he was bleeding heavily. In *The Telegraph*, George Allen reported the two women on the train, Mrs O'Connor and Miss Smith, were watching the drama from their carriage. They begged Hare not to go back to the fray but he tried to fight on, 'his reappearance being a fresh signal for firing a volley, and the air was soon filled with smoke'. But Hare became faint from blood loss and had to withdraw from the battle. Leadership was handed to Sub-Inspector O'Connor and Senior Constable Kelly, and the police continued to pour a hail of lead into the flimsy weatherboards of Ann Jones' inn.

Ned believed he was invincible in his iron suit. His disembodied voice rang out from behind his iron helmet. 'Fire away, you bloody dogs, you can't hurt us!' he shouted.

He could not have been more wrong. A policeman, Constable Charles Gascoigne, fired his Martini-Henry rifle and the heavy slug smashed into Ned's left arm. The arm was bent in a V shape to support the rifle stock and the bullet passed through the forearm, scoring the bone, before tearing into the bicep. Then another bullet ripped into the front of Ned's foot. These were horrific wounds that should have put him out of the battle. And then things got worse when Joe Byrne was hit in the right leg. It was a bad injury that might have broken the bone but Joe was able to retreat to the hotel and continue fighting. Apart from Hare, the only police casualty was one of the Aboriginal troopers, who suffered a minor head wound. The first round had been won by the police.

Inside the hotel it was a hellish scene. The terrified hostages huddled on top of each other on the floor as bullets smashed holes in the walls. Some of the prisoners sheltered beneath furniture or behind the brick fireplaces. Three men—John Larkin, Andrew Rowan and William Sandercook—crouched behind bags of grain in the kitchen. Older children hid under beds, the younger ones were wrapped up in their parents' arms. In one crowded minute, an estimated sixty shots ripped into the tiny building. The windows shattered and bottles and glasses were blasted apart. Chunks of splintered wood and shards of glass flew through the rooms. The screams and prayers of the prisoners could be heard over the roar of gunfire. There was a stench of fear, gunsmoke and spilt spirits. The House of Sport had become a killing zone.

The gang returned fire, drawing a new volley from the besieging police. And then a wail of agony cut through the darkness. It was young Johnny Jones. A police bullet had smashed through the wall and into frail Johnny, just above his hip. Mortally wounded, he screamed for help. 'Oh, mother! I am shot!' Then another bullet ricocheted off a wall and grazed Jane Jones' forehead. Blood poured down her face but the wound was not as serious as it looked. Desperately, Ann and Jane carried Johnny to the residence, where Ann's youngest boys had been locked in a bedroom.

Nineteen-year-old David Mortimer, who only hours earlier had been calling the quadrilles for a merry bush dance, said in a statement to the police that he could not bear to hear Johnny Jones' screams:

I put my fingers into my ears so as not to hear his screams of agony and the lamentations of his mother. We could do nothing and the bullets continued to whistle through the building.

Another hostage, a farmer named Robert Gibbons, said: 'The bullets rattled through the side of the house and we had to lie down. We were packed so close we had to lie on our sides.' Young Thomas Cameron wrote in a letter to his brother:

I can tell you it was something awful. The room I was in was fairly riddled with balls coming in all directions breaking the clock on the mantelpiece and coming through the windows and hitting the table and sofa.

There were periodic lulls in the gunfire and Ann's grief-stricken cries could be heard cutting through the night as her son's lifeblood poured onto the kitchen floor. At times she ran shrieking from the kitchen and into the bush before returning to the mortally wounded Johnny. It was a miracle that she escaped the bullets. Eventually a labourer named Jack McHugh—'a jolly Irishman'—desperately scooped up the wounded boy and carried him through the fire zone to safety at the Reardons' home. It was one of the bravest and least recognised acts of the Glenrowan siege.

When Ann and Jane were released several hours later, they took Johnny by train to hospital in Wangaratta and were there when he died the next day. The siege continued as Ann waited by Johnny's bedside and she was still in Wangaratta when her home and business were burnt to the ground. Thirty years after the siege she told the journalist Brian Cookson that her memories made her 'miserable unto death'.

> The police kept on shooting and no-one knew who would be the next to fall. The bullets were doing the outlaws no harm at all. The police might have rushed the place easily and captured them—if they had been men enough. But they were not men. They lay there in safety and kept firing at the house.

When Ann recounted the death of Johnny she broke into a fit of sobbing. Three decades had passed but the pain had not dimmed.

There were other casualties of the police assault. Martin Cherry was a fifty-eight-year-old Irishman who worked on the railways. It is believed he went to the inn after hearing Ned Kelly was there, saying, 'I don't believe it—I will go and see.' His curiosity cost him his life. Cherry was sheltering in the kitchen when a bullet cut through the wall and hit him in the groin. Terribly wounded, he lived long enough to receive the last sacraments from Father Gibney the next day and died moments later. The police tried to encourage a belief that Ned had shot Cherry but there is no doubt that it was a police bullet that killed the Irishman. An inquest later found Martin Cherry, 'a quiet, harmless old man', died of a gunshot wound, 'but no blame can be attached to any member of the police force'.

George Metcalf was one of Piazzi's road workers. George was trying to shelter behind one of Ann's chimneys when the bullets started to fly. One smashed into the chimney, sending shards of brick into his eyes. He died of his injuries several months later. Michael Reardon was the son of Margaret and James, the platelayer who had been made to rip up the rail line. Seventeen-year-old Michael was shot in the shoulder by Sergeant Steele as the Reardon family tried to flee from the besieged inn. Michael lived for another sixty years but always carried the lead slug in his body. Jane Jones' head wound was not serious but she died of tuberculosis two years after the siege. Ann claimed Jane died from a combination of the effects of the wound and grief for her brother.

As the gunfight continued, Ned's fourteen-year-old cousin Jack Lloyd was in an agony of indecision. He had been given the job of firing the Chinese rockets to signal the start of the uprising when the train crashed but it was now clear the plot was failing. Crouched in the darkness at the front of McDonnell's Hotel, Jack made his decision. He fired the rockets and bright green flares exploded in the night sky. Suddenly, Ned was in an even more difficult position; the flares would send the sympathisers to a pre-arranged meeting point. Badly wounded, he would have to leave the inn to contact the sympathisers and warn them the revolt had collapsed.

It was now almost three-thirty in the morning. The police had formed a quarter-circle around the front and parlour sides of the inn and sporadic bursts of gunfire continued. The bush-rangers returned fire from the hotel and, as the archaeology later proved, occasionally reloaded in the relative safety of the western bedroom. More police had arrived from Wangaratta and the hostages were still pinned down on the floor. Then the firing died off for a while and some of the women and children fled to safety. The Reardons and their six children were delayed, how-ever, because their eldest daughter Catherine was badly cramped from hiding under a bed. Eventually the family crept away from the inn in darkness. A voice called: 'Who comes there?' 'Women and children!' the Reardons shouted in reply but, hearing the male voices of James and Michael Reardon, the police responded with a volley of shots. Three of the children reached safety and the rest of the family ran back to the inn.

Ned was also waiting for his chance to escape and warn the sympathisers. The gang was still holed up in the pub when a policeman, Constable William Phillips, crept around the parlour on the western side to the rear of the inn. As he crouched in the darkness, Phillips could hear voices from inside the building. The voices were those of Ned and Joe. Unable to see his targets, who were standing in the darkened breezeway, the policeman could only listen as a remarkable discussion unfolded between the bushrangers. It was one of the most revealing moments of the siege and, 128 years later, the archaeologists would uncover sensational evidence that could be linked to this final conversa-tion between Ned and his mate.

Ned: 'Come with me and load my rifle. I'm cooked.'

Joe: 'So am I. I think my leg is broke.'

Ned: 'Leg be damned. You've got the use of your arms. Come on. Load for me. I'll pink the buggers.'

Joe's reply highlighted the terrible position the gang was in: 'Don't be so excited. The boys will hear us and it'll dishearten them.'

Ned: 'I'm afraid it's a case with us this time.'

Joe: 'Well, it's your fault. I always said this bloody armour would bring us to grief.'

Ned suddenly sparked up: 'Don't you believe it. Old Hare is cooked and we'll soon finish the rest.'

Joe cursed as he hobbled back to the bar, still wearing his suit of iron. Ned left the building again. Terribly wounded and faced with certain defeat, he would fight on. But Joe was right. The armour in which Ned had placed so much faith had failed him, at least for now. The supporters, however, were still out there ready to rise up. The battle was not over yet. Bleeding heavily, Ned limped out into the open and exchanged more shots with the police. Constable Gascoigne returned fire. Still convinced of the power of his armour, Ned shouted: 'You bloody cocktails, you can't hurt me! I'm in iron!'

His mare was tethered beyond Ann's stables at the back of the site. He needed to ride to his friends and warn them to call off the uprising but before he could mount, he fell to his knees. Blood was pouring from his ruined left arm and he could barely walk. He took off his helmet and removed a waterproof silk cap that covered his head. He put the cap under his elbow and it quickly filled with blood. Then Ned put the helmet back on but left the cap on the ground with his rifle. The old Colt was now so clogged with blood it would not work. He would never fire it again.

Ned met up with Tom Lloyd in the darkness and they made their way to the meeting point. It's not known how many sympathisers had gathered there. In *A Short Life*, Ian Jones wrote that one witness believed there were 150 men there but another put the number at thirty. In any case, Ned would have had forces at least equal to the police and could have won the battle—but he knew the cause was lost. He warned the sympathisers not to join the fight and they faded into the bush. 'This is our fight,' he said. 'I am prepared to die.' Then he crept back to the inn. He could still have escaped—but he would not leave without attempting to rescue Joe, Dan and Steve.

It was now just after five o'clock on the morning of the twenty-eighth. There was another break in the fighting and more of the women and children dashed to safety out of the inn. Johnny Jones still lay mortally wounded in the kitchen. Ann continued to wander in and out of the building, screaming abuse at the police. 'Cowards!' she shouted. 'Murdering hounds!' The reporter McWhirter recalled: 'She was calling them murderers and said Ned Kelly was man enough for any of them. She just heaped one abuse on the back of the other.'

The Reardons tried to escape a second time. Margaret Reardon would later say Dan Kelly had told her to leave the inn and to tell the police not to shoot until the hostages were safe. She screamed into the dark morning for mercy and a voice she recognised as Sergeant Steele's shouted in reply: 'Put up your hands and come this way or I will shoot you like bloody dogs.' Margaret put baby Bridget under her arm and advanced in the darkness, but Sergeant Steele 'kept on firing against us'. A slug from Steele's shotgun ripped through the rug that was keeping the baby warm. Amazingly, it grazed the little girl's forehead but did not cause serious injury. Another policeman, Constable James Arthur, was furious with Steele and later told the Royal Commission that he warned the sergeant: 'If you fire at that woman again I'm damned if I won't shoot at you.'

Margaret reached safety with three of her children but her husband and two of the children fled back to the inn. The trigger-happy Steele turned his attentions to them. He fired both barrels of his shotgun. One shot bored into Michael's back and lodged in his shoulder, near a lung. The teenager collapsed through the inn's back door while Joe Byrne loosed off some shots from the bar-room window. James Reardon would later say the injury had rendered his son 'quite useless'.

Dawn was less than an hour away when Ned returned to the inn. As he crept through the back door he saw the armoured figure of Joe standing at the bar, glass of whiskey in hand. Their eyes met and Joe raised the glass to his mate, shouting a defiant toast: 'Many more years in the bush for the Kelly Gang!'

At that instant, a hail of bullets crashed through the front of the inn. A slug found the exposed flesh below Joe's breastplate, and tore into his thigh. It severed his femoral artery and, in a great gush of blood, he slumped to the floor. James Reardon heard him fall and later described it to the Royal Commission.

Byrne had been shot at the end of the counter, going from the passage. He was standing still. I only heard him fall. I heard him fall like a log, and he never groaned or anything, and I could hear a sound like blood gushing. That was about five or six in the morning; but when I was coming out, the other two [Dan Kelly and Steve Hart] were both standing close together in the passage, with the butt end of their rifles on the ground. They were struck while I was there; I could hear the bullets flying off the armour several times. Their lives were saved for the time being by the armour.

Joe had died even before he could finish his drink. Twenty-three-year-old Joe had sworn to fight with Ned to the death and he fulfilled his oath. Opium-smoking, hard-drinking, good-time

Joe was dead in a lake of blood and Ned had lost his lieuten-ant and best mate. It was the beginning of the end for the Kelly Gang. There would be no more years in the bush for any of them.

Grief-stricken, Ned said to Dan and Steve: 'We're done. We had better get away.' Then he limped to the verandah and shouted a challenge to the police. There was no reply. When he got back inside Dan and Steve had disappeared into a bedroom. Believing his brother and mate had 'cleared out' Ned crept out the back door. It was past six in the morning and a heavy mist hung in the pre-dawn air. Ned would fight it out one more time. What he had already done would have been enough to cement his place in history. But what really propelled him into folklore was that he did it in a suit of iron armour. The armour is the image that defines him and more than a century later we still don't fully understand it.

15

MEN OF STEEL

'A damn good blacksmith'

In colonial times, the Glenrowan blacksmith's workshop was one of the busiest and most important businesses in town. The smith worked from a forge diagonally opposite the inn on Beaconsfield Parade, turning out horseshoes, farming equipment and household goods. Like all of the town's original buildings, the workshop has now vanished, but unlike most small towns today, Glenrowan still has a professional blacksmith.

Gary Nicholls works in a tin workshop on Siege Street, a few doors up from the inn site and just metres from where Ned fell. Nicholls can make horseshoes and farming tools but his specialty is armour. He makes authentic reproductions from 1.5- or 3-millimetre-thick steel. He heats the metal to a cherry red glow in a forge and bangs it into shape with heavy hammers. When it is bolted and strapped together, divots are thumped into the heavy steel to replicate the bullet marks left in Ned's suit—and another piece of Kellyana is ready for the tourism market.

The demand for Nicholls' suits, and those made by other smiths, reflects the immense fascination with the Kelly armour. Of all the imagery of the gang, it is the armour in all its glorious successes and failures that fascinates and keeps the myth not only alive but growing.

Adam Ford investigates how the armour might have been made. Courtesy Reece Rayner and Neal Kelly.

There have been many stories about the armour, some intriguing but impossible to prove. It has long been rumoured that multiple suits were made in the lead-up to the siege. Small sections of iron were found in a cave in the Woolshed Valley in the 1940s and some people believe these were part of an undiscovered fifth or even sixth set. Local people still hand down stories of an entire suit lying at the bottom of a farm dam near the Eleven Mile Creek at Greta. It has been said that a farmer found another suit buried in a paddock sixty years ago and has kept it hidden ever since. There were also reports that another set was made from saw blades after the siege and then dumped in the bush.

Unless another suit is found, it is impossible to say whether the stories are true. They appear to be more Kelly mythology, yet they cannot be dismissed. The original suits were made in secrecy and for obvious reasons no records were kept of their construction. It is feasible that more suits were made. If so, it was kept a secret then and is still a secret now.

There is much more that we do not know about the armour. Who made it? Where was it made and how? And perhaps more importantly, why was it made? Part of the answer to the last question lies in the widely held belief that the gang intended to use it for protection as they massacred the police in the wreckage of the train but this theory does not stand up well to examination. If the train had crashed, most of the people on board would have been killed or maimed. It is hard to see how the surviving police could have returned effective fire from the carnage of the gully, and even if they had, it would have been easier for the gang to pick off the injured survivors from behind the cover of a tree. In this clinical dispatching of human life, the armour would have been more hindrance than help.

Ned admitted the armour was made so he could 'paste the traps' but he also said it would enable him to rob banks without the risk of having to shoot anybody. There is little doubt he intended to rob the bank at Benalla after the train crash and it seems logical that the armour—which was not designed for a running gunbattle—could have been more effectively used in a bank hold-up. We will never know, but it is entirely possible that it was built for robbery, not mass murder.

The question that Ned did not answer was how he came up with the idea in the first place. Ian Jones thinks it might have come from the nineteenth-century romantic novel *Lorna Doone*. It told of the outlawed Doone clan— men riding 'with leather jerkins, and long boots, and iron plates on breast and head, plunder heaped behind their saddles, and flagons slung in front of them'. Ned had read the tale of chivalry and honour, and Jones believes it appealed deeply to him, inspiring the construction of a new type of armour that would repel not just swords and spears, but also bullets. There are other theories, though. In 1878, a Chinese miner wore a suit of mediaeval

Japanese armour in a parade in Beechworth, and it is thought that sight might have prompted Ned to make his own bullet-proof suit. Alternatively, a visit to Melbourne by an armoured American Civil War battleship might also have planted the seed in Ned's mind. It could have been any of these things, or a combination of them. Ned never said why he first thought of making the armour but we can say with certainty that it was his idea.

The historian Alex McDermott agrees the armour is reflective of Ned's personality and character but believes it also demonstrates a failure in planning. McDermott says the armour has often been described as a strategic masterstroke when in fact it was a disaster. The armour weighed more than a sack of wheat, made mounting a horse very difficult and severely restricted the wearer's ability to fire a rifle or pistol. The heavy steel certainly stopped a rifle bullet but it had a fundamental weakness; it provided no protection to the legs and arms. It was glamorous and romantic but of limited use in a gunbattle—a lesson Ned would learn in the harshest way. McDermott says:

> I'm struck by the psychology of the armour. I suspect that it suited a man like Kelly whose psychological makeup was such that he would confront anyone who crossed him or threatened him. He wasn't psychologically built for just hiding away and I reckon there's a part of Ned that wanted to stand up and say, 'you can't touch me, you can't take me down'.

Ned shouted as much to his police attackers during the siege. 'You can't hurt me, you dogs! I'm in iron!' he cried.

He had faith in the invincibility of his iron suit even after it had already failed him. But if the armour was the product of a deeply-rooted part of Ned's psyche or if he simply saw it as a tool to achieve his aims is open to debate.

It is known that work on the armour started in 1879 when sympathetic farmers began donating used mouldboards from their ploughs to the gang. Later, other farmers started to notice that mouldboards were going missing. Even in a time where theft was common, the disappearing mouldboards were puzzling. Who would need heavy mouldboards so badly that they would steal them? The answer of course was Ned Kelly, who was turning ploughs not into swords, but bulletproof armour.

It should have come as no surprise to the police. A police spy named Daniel Kennedy (codenamed 'The Diseased Stock Agent') had actually reported the mouldboard thefts and even told police that the boards would be used to make bullet-proof armour. In one of the greatest of the police blunders, the informant's reports were dismissed, and so was Kennedy. Refusing to believe the incredible tale, the police promptly sacked their most effective spy.

The Kellys were reasonable bush blacksmiths and some people think the suits were actually made by Ned and his men. The blacksmith Gary Nicholls takes his hat off to whoever made the suits, but he does not think the gang could have made them without help. Nicholls recently tried to make a suit out of modern mouldboards but found the steel shattered when he tried to hammer it. He thinks the steel in the Kellys' time must have been softer than today's but he remains full of admiration for whoever made the suits. 'Really, to put those suits of armour together was an incredible feat although personally I think there must have been a professional black-smith involved,' he said.

The suits are fine works. Each weighs around 45 kilograms and the parts fit together with precision. There are slight differences, especially in the shape of the eye slots, but all consist of helmets, breastplates, backplates and iron aprons to protect the groin. Ned's had shoulder plates for extra protection. They were also made to size. Ned's is the biggest to fit his large frame and the suit made for Steve—the former jockey—is the smallest. After the siege, many of the pieces were jumbled up and it was only recently that the components were assembled in the right order. Ned's suit is in a glass display box at the State Library of Victoria and Joe's is privately owned. Victoria Police owns Dan's and Steve's suits and they are on display at the Police Museum in Melbourne.

For years it was thought the quality of workmanship was so high that the suits must have been made in a blacksmith's shop in a town or village—a risky business that could land the maker in gaol. It has since been established, however, that at least one suit was made at an isolated forge—further testament to the maker's skill. We know this because Joe Byrne's suit was examined very closely by experts in 2003.

Scientists from the Australian Nuclear Science and Technology Organisation (ANSTO), with help from the University of Canberra and the National Museum of Australia, subjected Joe's suit to scientific tests including neutron scattering and X-rays. They confirmed that Joe's armour dated back to the late nineteenth century and was probably made of plough mouldboards. They also answered the big question—was the suit made in a blacksmith's forge or in the bush? The tests showed Joe Byrne's armour had been heated to around 750 degrees Celsius, consistent with the temperatures that would have been produced by a bush forge. Also, parts of the metal had been very hot while others were shaped relatively cold, further evidence of an outdoor forge. A professional blacksmith's shop could be all but ruled out.

The science tallied with local folklore, which has always maintained the suits were made at a secret place in the bush. According to the Lloyd family, Ned's suit was shaped over stripped logs and the ends of the logs were submerged in a creek to dull the sound of hammer on steel. This story fit evidence from Joseph Ashmead, Dan Kelly's childhood friend, who wrote in *The Briars and Thorns* that he tried on Ned's suit after the siege 'and saw distinctly the stain of sap from a green tree'. Ashmead said the suits were made by a local farmer in a bush forge at a secret place called Devil's Basin. What the scientists could not say was where that forge might have been.

A Beechworth prospector and amateur historian, Darren Sutton, believes he has found that answer, or at least part of it. After devastating bushfires scorched the Beechworth region in 2003, Sutton found the remains of a bush forge in the charred scrub, not far from the site of the Byrne homestead in the Woolshed Valley. To the untrained eye, there was not much to see, but an informed examination of the area shows pieces of a jigsaw that can be fitted together to prove that there was once a forge in the area.

A jumble of scattered bricks is evidence of the forge itself and Sutton believes the scatter pattern of the bricks shows that they were deliberately kicked down when the smiths were finished. Pieces of worked iron still remain on the site and clinkers—the by-product of heated coking coal—show the forge was heated to temperatures of around 800 degrees. This was a little hotter than the temperature estimate in the ANSTO testing, but it falls within a margin of error. The undergrowth concealed a line of stump holes showing the remains of a crude building with a raised floor. Sutton also found metalworking tools at the site, including a rough chisel and a punch. Also hidden in the grass was the rusted, perforated metal base of a gold pan. These discoveries were proof that Darren Sutton had uncovered the remains of a blacksmith's forge that had been operating in the bush more than a century ago.

Most importantly, Sutton found a rather innocuous-looking piece of rusty, curved iron about 30 centimetres long. This piece of metal had two mounting holes punched in the base, indicating it was once a piece of plough mouldboard. As soon as he saw the discarded scrap of iron in the burnt ground, Sutton was intrigued. He called upon Ian Jones for help and both men came to the conclusion that it was a section of the bottom of Joe Byrne's breastplate that had been cut away because it was too long. Cut marks on the iron matched the blade of the chisel Sutton found at the scene, proving that this tool had been used to cut the metal.

Sutton then compared the piece of iron to the bottom of the breastplate on a replica of Joe's armour at the Benalla museum. He said a shiver went down his spine; the offcut was a perfect match to the replica. He believed he had solved one of the enduring mysteries of the Kelly story—where and how at least one suit of armour was made.

Sutton believed two men made Joe's armour, the Beechworth blacksmiths Charlie Knight and Tom Straughair. It would have taken two to three weeks to complete and it is likely that

Joe would have visited the forge to check on progress and try on his new suit for size. Darren Sutton believes it was one of these tryouts that prompted his iron tailors to remove the bottom of the breastplate and throw the offcut away. For the prospector, it was a defining moment.

I always knew Joe's armour was made near where he lived in the Woolshed Valley and the other three suits were made near Greta.

It means we can dispel the myths about the armour and prove that it was made by a damned good black-smith and not by an amateur. We can now say 'this is Joe Byrne's suit, this is where it was made, this is how it was made and here are the tools that were used to make it'. It's about putting history right.

Darren Sutton thought his discovery had filled in one of the most important gaps in the story, but he was in for some disappointment. The iron scrap was sent away for comparison with Joe Byrne's original armour and the results were devastating. Metal-testing showed the samples did not match and the state heritage agency, Heritage Victoria, said Darren Sutton's sample was not part of the Kelly armour. The authority's senior archaeologist, Jeremy Smith, had visited the forge site and agreed Sutton had a good circumstantial case, but the metal-testing confirmed the two samples were from separate pieces of steel. Unless new evidence emerges, 'the case is closed'.

Darren Sutton, however, remains convinced he has found the forge where Joe Byrne's armour was made. He believes the metal-testing was flawed and that further testing would prove he is right. Once again, a Kelly story has provided two sides, plenty of intrigue and a lack of conclusive proof. Sutton has influential support from Ian Jones, however, who became convinced after inspecting the bush forge. Jones was sceptical at first but the forge intrigued him. When he checked his records, he found the mounting holes in Sutton's offcut matched those in Dan Kelly's armour. Jones now believes the metal-testing was inaccurate because Sutton's sample was deeply scored by the testers, while only a tiny layer of metal was removed from Joe Byrne's original suit.

Jones and Sutton are certain that more rigorous testing will confirm Joe's armour was made at the Woolshed Valley forge. They now hope to find a suspected forge site behind the Bald Hill at Greta, where they believe Ned's suit was made.

In August 2010, all four original suits of armour were brought to Beechworth for the town's annual Ned Kelly Weekend. It was only the fourth time that the complete set had been reunited since 1880. For Darren Sutton, it was a chance to compare his metal sample to Joe Byrne's original suit. Under strict security, Sutton was allowed to place his sample directly against the bottom of Joe's breastplate. The pieces fit together like a jigsaw puzzle.

Photographs show Sutton's sample in perfect alignment with the bottom left of Joe's breastplate. There is a slight gap between the plate and the offcut (Sutton thinks this was caused by fracturing of the metal when the piece was severed) but otherwise the two pieces fit together as if they had been made from the same mould. If there really is no connection between Joe's suit and Darren Sutton's sample, then we have to wonder about the odds of a random piece of metal from an old bush forge matching perfectly the breastplate of Joe Byrne's armour.

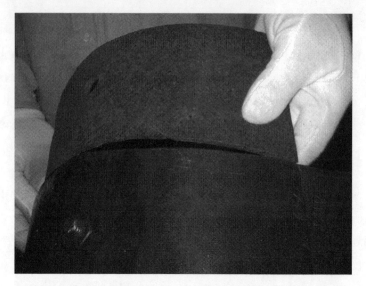

Darren Sutton's armour sample matches Joe Byrne's suit.
Image courtesy of Tania Sutton.

It is compelling evidence but it is hard to argue with science. It will take more testing to confirm or disprove Sutton's theory. Until then, the location of the bush smithy where history was forged will remain a topic of debate. We may also never know who made the suits. The Beechworth blacksmiths Straughair and Knight are good candidates but for obvious reasons they did not sign their names to their creations and might never be confirmed as the smiths who built national treasures.

More than thirty years after the siege, the journalist Brian Cookson tried to shed new light on the armour story when an elderly Glenrowan resident dropped in to the Sydney *Sun* offices with an intriguing story. William Grovener spoke at length to Cookson—a conversation the journalist said finally settled 'definitely and beyond question how, where and by whom the armour was made'.

Grovener said Ned had told his brother Jim all about the armour. It had been Ned's idea to manufacture the suits to protect the gang against a chance shot by the police. The gang tried all sorts of metal, including circular saw blades, but none of it would stop a bullet. Then Ned, 'a first-class blacksmith', came up with the idea of mouldboards and oversaw the construction of the suits at a bush forge near the family's Greta homestead. The old man told Cookson:

> They had plenty of friends, all farmers, and worn-out plough shares were by no means scarce. Whilst the police were looking in all sorts of unlikely places the outlaws—working under Ned's direction—were busy at the bush smithy manufacturing the heavy defences that stood them in such valuable stead later on in their desperate career.

Although Grovenor was only passing on hearsay, his story was intriguing. It also tallies with the later scientific testing that indicated the suits were made in the bush. It is hard, however, to believe that Ned was the master smith. He—or they—will probably never get the credit the work so richly deserves.

16

THE LAST STAND

'The most extraordinary sight'

The key players in the gunfight are commemorated with statues at important sites across the siege precinct. Painted wooden Aboriginal troopers (erroneously clad in uniform) approach the inn while two bushrangers in armour stand at the front fence. They must be Dan and Steve, Joe having already died in the shootout. Father Gibney stands on the railway platform, clutching a Bible to his chest. There are two well-dressed women on the platform. Presumably they are meant to be Sub-Inspector O'Connor's wife and her sister but they played only a minor role in the story and it is hard to understand why they are included. Alternatively, they could represent Ann and Jane but if so, their placement at the railway station is puzzling. There are no statues representing either the reporters or the hostages. Thomas Curnow, in particular, is notably absent.

Ned is represented near where he fell just to the east of the inn at the end of his Last Stand. This Ned is made of logs. He is seated on the ground, leaning against a large dead stump, with his legs protruding stiffly from the apron of his armour. Red painted blood stains his legs. He is still wearing his helmet and behind the eye-slit he looks a little cross-eyed. For one so wooden, this Ned still manages to seem a little aggrieved at this indignity.

The exact spot where Ned fell is open to debate but the accepted place between the inn and the 1888 police station is a good approximation. The precise spot does not really matter. What does matter is gaining an understanding of how the Last Stand played out because, of all the amazing moments in Ned's life, it was this one that most defined him. Right up until the last minute, he could have escaped into the bush but instead he decided to fight on in a hopeless attempt to rescue Dan and Steve. Even as it happened, observers noted Ned's loyalty and determination. The seeds of romance were sown immediately in accounts in the media.

McWhirter, who witnessed the drama unfold, reported in *The Age*, 'it was not the intention of the bold ruffian to desert his comrades'. The policeman Francis Hare later disagreed: 'This is quite wrong. Kelly being wounded tried to escape on foot but being shot in the foot was unable to walk.' But it was Hare who was incorrect. 'The bold ruffian' could walk, albeit with a limp, and had in fact decided not to escape but to fight on, and it would cost his life.

When he fell with shattered limbs, Ned was defeated but in some ways ultimately victorious. It gave us the saying 'as game as Ned Kelly', which eventually came to embody how Australians see themselves—brave, independent and fiercely loyal to their mates. Mateship is not exclusive to Australia, but Ned Kelly is, and on that cold morning Ned showed a depth of character that would inspire Australians through war and the Depression and into a new future.

Dressed in his armour covered by an overcoat, Ned had left the inn for the last time soon after Joe Byrne was shot. It was a superhuman effort to walk, let alone fight. His left arm was shattered in two places and his right foot was badly torn. He had already lost a lot of blood. Weighed down by 45 kilograms of iron, he slipped past the police in the pre-dawn darkness and tried to mount his horse, which was tied up near the stables. Constable Gascoigne later said he saw the horse rear up and trot away. Heavily armoured and badly wounded, Ned would fight his last battle on foot.

Ned Kelly at bay, drawn by Mr T Carrington during the encounter, 1880.
Image courtesy of the Pictures Collection, State Library of Victoria.

He hobbled up the slope behind the inn and again met his cousin Tom Lloyd. It was then that Ned realised Dan and Steve were still at the inn. Reeling from loss of blood, Ned fainted for a moment. When he came to, Tom helped Ned load three revolvers. They said their farewells and Ned struggled to his feet. Armed with the revolvers and a faith in his iron suit, he limped back towards the inn to rescue his brother and mate. A winter mist cloaked the frozen ground as Ned lurched through the scrub, weighed down by injury, loss and the massive bulk of his armour.

The odds were already overwhelming. More police reinforcements had arrived and anyone with a gun and enough pluck could take a shot at capturing Ned or his comrades. The gang members were worth £2000 each, dead or alive. Police and civilians were eligible for a share of the reward and now a growing force of armed men was intent on the capture of Ned Kelly.

The next man to see Ned was Constable Arthur, who was stunned at the sight of this tall, unworldly figure clanking through the mist. It was of human shape, yet impossibly tall and bulky. But it was a man, and he was armed with loaded revolvers. Ned swept aside his coat, exposing a pistol to Arthur and the policeman fired a shot from his rifle straight at the figure's head.

A Martini-Henry rifle discharges with a deafening bang. In a cloud of smoke, the large, soft lead bullet flies at about 400 metres per second and tends to flatten on impact, causing severe injuries. The bullet from Arthur's rifle cracked into Ned's iron helmet, leaving a deep divot. The policeman could not believe his eyes. The giant figure should have dropped like a stone. Instead, it reeled but still stood—and then it fired back!

The stunned Arthur kept shooting. One more bullet and then another slammed into the monstrous apparition and although it staggered again, still it remained upright.

It rapped the butt of its pistol against the iron breastplate, creating an eerie ringing as the figure continued to stagger forwards. A voice rang out from behind the iron mask. 'Fire away you bastards! You cannot hurt me!'

In one sense Ned was right. The armour in which he had placed so much faith had worked. It protected him from the bullets but in another way it also proved his undoing. He could not turn and flee, and his vision of the battle was limited to the narrow slot of the helmet. It was difficult to aim effectively and his ruined left arm meant he could barely reload his pistols. Like a great, blind tank he rumbled through the bush, firing with little effect and absorbing one hammer blow after another.

As he staggered towards the inn, he shouted to his brother and mate still holed up inside. Dan and Steve appeared in the breezeway behind the hotel and fired a volley. The policemen ducked for cover as bark and leaves flew off the trees and still Ned stumbled on, trying to reach his trapped mates. Some of the attackers feared they were battling a creature from another world, a monster that was impervious to bullets. One policeman, Senior Constable Kelly, yelled out, 'He's the bunyip!' but later said the word he used was 'bulletproof'. Hare later wrote: 'He [Ned] appeared to be a fiend with a charmed life.'

The reporters who witnessed this amazing moment drew upon literature in an attempt to capture the outlandish image they had seen. Thomas Carrington wrote that the strange figure 'looked for all the world like the ghost of Hamlet's father with no head, only a very long, thin neck'. George Allen recalled

Dumas' *The Man in the Iron Mask*. Both reporters described how bullets cannoned into the figure without effect while the sound of the revolver butt striking the armour rang out like a bell in the crisp morning air. Carrington wrote: 'It was the most extraordinary sight I ever saw or read of in my life, and I felt fairly spellbound with wonder, and I could not stir or speak.'

Meanwhile, Ned sat down next to a tree stump and awkwardly reloaded his last revolver. Painfully, he got to his feet and lurched closer to his impossible goal of reaching the inn and his stranded mates.

Thomas Carrington later told of seeing 'a man in a small, round, tweed cap stealing up on the left of the figure'. This was Sergeant Steele. At about the same time, a railway guard named Jesse Dowsett joined the fray. A superstitious character, Dowsett thought he was fighting with Satan himself. Dowsett later told the press that he fired five or six shots at the armoured figure and 'I heard the bullets scud off him'. Another bullet bounced off the figure's head 'like a parched pea'. Dowsett cried to the nearby police, 'That man must be the devil.' He steadied his revolver and fired at Ned from close range. 'How do you like that, old man?' Dowsett asked. Ned returned the question, punctuated with a gunshot, 'How do you like *this*?' The bullet whistled past Dowsett.

There was a policeman between Ned and the hotel. It was the shotgun-wielding Sergeant Steele who had fired so madly at the fleeing Reardon family. Ned and Steele exchanged shots and Steele dived to the ground, feigning a hit. Then, from a distance of just a few yards, Steele realised at last that it was a man in an iron suit. He reloaded and fired both barrels of his shotgun at Ned's exposed legs.

Terribly wounded, heartsick and dizzy from the loss of blood, these final shots brought Ned crashing to the ground. 'I am done! I am done!' he cried in despair. Constable Kelly then sprang forward and wrenched the iron helmet from the bushranger's head. 'By God! It's Ned!' cried Steele, at the same time grabbing Ned by the wrist. The bushranger's revolver discharged for the last time and the bullet blew Steele's tweed hat from his head.

'I said I would be in at your death, you wretch!' Steele yelled. At that moment, Constable Dwyer tried to kick the fallen bushranger. Unfortunately for Dwyer, his shin connected with the armour and did more harm to his leg than to Ned. But Steele's blood was up and he raised his weapon to fire. Ned could have died in that instant, yet he was to live another twenty weeks, thanks to the brave Constable Hugh Bracken. The Glenrowan policeman raised his shotgun. 'I'll shoot any bloody man that dares touch him,' he warned, and Steele withdrew.

Dan Kelly and Steve Hart were still holed up in the breezeway between the inn and Ann's home. Enraged at Ned's fall, they fired another volley of shots. Again, the bullets missed their mark, shredding bark and leaves from the trees, and again the police returned fire. Yet more bullets tore into the battered inn, and one struck Dan in the leg as he ducked back inside. This injury would later help to identify Dan's body, providing strong evidence against the myth that he and Steve survived the siege.

It was just after seven-thirty in the morning. Ned was stripped of his armour and of his mystique. Bleeding and near death, he hobbled under guard to the railway station, where he would wait for a train to deliver him to justice. The uprising had failed and Ned's reign over the wilds of Kelly Country was over.

THE CAPTURE OF NED KELLY.

The Capture of Ned Kelly, wood engraving created 3 July 1880 by Julian Ashton. Image courtesy of the Pictures Collection, State Library of Victoria.

The man who had enraged the authorities, inspired the down-trodden and enthralled the press was a prisoner, brought down by his own bravery and his faith in the armour he thought would save him. The Last Stand was over.

The original Glenrowan train station was dismantled in the 1940s and the platform left bare for a while. Eventually, a replica station, complete with stationmaster's office, was built on or near the site of the first one and this neat, painted weatherboard building is now a key part of the siege precinct for tourists trying to get an understanding of the Last Stand. Ned was taken to the office after his capture. It was felt that he might die there of his wounds but he was not willing to give up, even in defeat.

A respected doctor from Benalla, John Nicholson, treated him and did enough to keep him alive to face trial. The doctor was one of the earliest Kelly 'treasure hunters' and the green and gold sash knotted around Ned's waist caught his eye. Doctor Nicholson was so taken with the sash that he took it for himself. It was sent to England for a while but to the credit of Nicholson's descendants, the sash was donated to the museum at Benalla in 1973. A newspaper at that time rather excitedly reported the re-discovery as 'one of the most exciting finds in history'. Hyperbole aside, it was a magnificent gift and it can now be seen, still stained with Ned's blood, in a glass case at the museum.

Reporters and police were able to speak to Ned as he lay on a stretcher in the train station. Superintendent Sadleir helped Ned to sip some brandy and asked if he could get his brother and friend to surrender. Rather unfairly, Ned said he no longer had faith in Dan and Steve as they were cowards. He did not complain of his terrible injuries but mentioned several times that he had cold feet. Thomas Carrington placed a kerosene tin with hot water next to Ned's feet to warm them up. Carrington took the opportunity to have several discussions with Ned and gained some interesting, if misleading, intelligence.

Carrington asked Ned about the armour and was told Ned had made it to 'paste as many of the traps' as he could. Ned also said the armour was made only for the upper parts of the body because the gang intended to barricade the hotel and fight from the windows. This seems highly unlikely because the gang had never planned a siege. Ned also took the opportunity to give Carrington some further misinformation that would lead to speculation over the decades. Carrington wrote:

He told me several times that Byrne, Dan Kelly and Hart had escaped, and that the only people in the hotel were those they'd stuck up. This, of course, was a lie, and what his object was in telling it, it is difficult to say.

The siege continued. Dan and Steve were still trapped inside the bullet-riddled hotel, firing occasionally to keep the police at bay. About thirty hostages were still stranded inside. At about ten o'clock a truce was called when a white handkerchief fluttered from a shattered window. The prisoners rushed from the inn, under the guns of the police. The McAuliffe brothers were arrested as sympathisers and with the other hostages, they were ordered to lie on the wet and frozen ground. Perhaps because he did not have to do it himself, this spectacle provided some level of entertainment to *The Telegraph* reporter George Allen. 'The scene presented when they were all lying on the ground, and demonstrating the respectability of their characters, was unique and in some degree amusing.'

The hotel was now empty but for Dan and Steve, and the mortally wounded Irishman Martin Cherry in the kitchen. By now, the bush telegraph had sent word of the drama throughout Kelly Country and hundreds of people—maybe as many as a thousand—had gathered in the town. The real telegraph had also sent word—thousands of words in fact—to Melbourne and Sydney, where newspaper readers were clamouring for news. More reporters and photographers arrived during the morning. Father Gibney, who would identify the bodies of Dan and Steve, arrived soon after midday, by which time the siege had entered an uneasy lull.

Amazingly, the police were cooking up a bizarre scheme to construct a bulletproof shield and had called in artillery with the aim of literally blowing the inn apart. A field gun was actually loaded onto a train in Melbourne to be sent north. When Thomas Carrington heard this news, he thought it was a joke. But this remarkable piece of overkill was never needed. The gun was an hour out of Melbourne when it was recalled; by then the siege was over.

In the meantime, though, the police were still unable to dislodge the last two outlaws. They came up with the idea of burning the building down and were preparing to do so when Ned's sisters, Maggie, Kate and Grace, arrived with Wild Wright. There was a simmering discontent among the crowd, many of whom were sympathisers, but the Kelly girls only had thoughts for their brother. The police asked Maggie to approach the inn and urge Dan and Steve to surrender but she replied she 'would sooner see them burned first'.

At this time, Senior Constable Charles Johnston from Violet Town calmly approached the hotel, braving gunfire from within, and set a bundle of kerosene-soaked straw against the outside of the parlour wall. He struck a match and within minutes the building began to burn. Maggie tried to reach the inn but was ordered back by the police. Flames could be seen through the parlour window as the calico in the ceiling caught fire. Sixteen-year-old Kate screamed for 'my poor, poor brother' as the flames burned higher.

Father Gibney, defying orders from the police, rushed into the burning building, where he found the body of Joe Byrne near the bar and those of Dan and Steve on the beds in the western bedroom. Flames were roaring through the ceiling

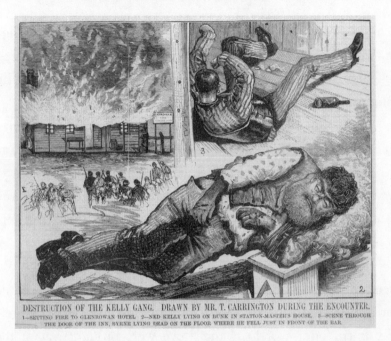

DESTRUCTION OF THE KELLY GANG. DRAWN BY MR. T. CARRINGTON DURING THE ENCOUNTER. 1—SETTING FIRE TO GLENROWAN HOTEL 2—NED KELLY LYING ON BUNK IN STATION-MASTER'S HOUSE. 3—SCENE THROUGH THE DOOR OF THE INN, BYRNE LYING DEAD ON THE FLOOR WHERE HE FELL JUST IN FRONT OF THE BAR.

Destruction of the Kelly Gang, drawn by Mr T Carrington during the encounter, 1880. Image courtesy of the Pictures Collection, State Library of Victoria.

now and Dan and Steve had to be left to burn. But Constable Armstrong—one of the four police who had behaved in such a timid fashion at the Sherritt hut some forty hours earlier— redeemed himself somewhat by helping Gibney to recover Joe's body from the floor. The 'jolly old Irishman' Martin Cherry was still in the kitchen, which was also starting to catch fire. He was taken outside and lived long enough to receive the last sacraments from Gibney. Cherry died moments later, the second innocent life lost in the siege.

A light breeze fanned the flames and the inn was raging. The ten gallons of spirits that Ann Jones had hoped to sell to her customers added to the inferno and explosions could be heard as the Kellys' ammunition popped in the heat. The roof fell in and the fire took hold of Ann's home behind the inn.

Onlookers gazed in awe and grief as the flames roared high into a grey winter's sky and the bodies inside were incinerated. Helpless, Ned lay wounded in the stationmaster's office as his plot for revolution went up in flames.

Soon, only the two brick chimneys and Ann's 'Best Accommodation' sign were standing. The rest was a charred and smoking ruin—all that was left of Ann Jones' dream of a better life. As her home and livelihood were lost to the flames, Ann was 25 kilometres away in Wangaratta, where she and Jane kept a bedside vigil and waited for Johnny to die.

The siege was over but the danger was not. The crowd was seething in grief and fury, and the police feared emotions could boil over into an explosive confrontation. When the horribly burnt bodies of Dan and Steve were brought out of the smouldering ruins a shock wave rippled through the muttering crowd. Newspapers reported that when Wild Wright led Maggie to the body believed to be that of Dan, she 'raised a dirge-like cry and wept bitterly'. The Kelly siblings were very close and it must have been a heart-rending moment.

The police wanted to keep the bodies for an inquest but more violence was brewing. Sympathisers had placed a barricade over the rail line to the south, isolating Glenrowan from rail traffic. The telegraph was still working but the wires could easily be pulled down. The police had some fifty men in town but they were vastly outnumbered and the rebellious rumblings of the crowd convinced them that discretion was the better part of valour. Superintendent Sadleir agreed to a request from Steve's brother Dick to release the bodies to the families. The remains of Dan and Steve were wrapped in blankets and taken to Maggie's house at Greta.

A wake was held at Maggie's that night. There were no journalists there but that did not stop them reporting that the wake was a riotous affair, with the Kelly family and supporters allegedly vowing revenge on the police. The grieving Kellys made it clear the bodies would not be surrendered and it was reported a large party of armed sympathisers was ready to keep the authorities back at gunpoint. The newspapers said, 'reports came from Greta that all the Kelly sympathisers had made themselves intoxicated at the wake, and were bouncing about armed, and threatening to attack the police'.

Another report said:

So great was the crush that Mrs. Skillion [sic] lost her temper, and seizing a gun hustled the crowd out, and then allowed them to view the remains in couples. Many of the male sympathisers were armed, and whilst in a drunken state professed to be anxious for a brush with the police.

The scenes of grief were terrible as dozens of people lined up to see the bodies. Tom Lloyd reportedly took Kate Kelly's hand and 'swore a most dreadful oath' of vengeance. But there was no trouble and Dan and Steve were laid to rest at Greta the next day. Joe's body was treated with less respect. His remains were taken, with Ned, by rail to Benalla and both were kept in the police lockup. The next day, Joe's body was strung up on the lockup door for the benefit of photographers. A gruesome image taken by photographer WT Lindt shows another photographer capturing an image of Joe hanging on the door. Joe Byrne's family did not claim his body and he was buried in an unmarked grave at Wangaratta.

Joe Byrne's body outside Benalla Police Station, 29 June 1880.
Photographer JW Lindt. Image courtesy of the Pictures Collection, State
Library of Victoria.

In *Ned Kelly's Last Days*, Alex C Castles and Jennifer Castles wrote that Joe's death certificate listed his occupation as 'outlaw'. Ned's was listed more benignly as 'labourer', giving Joe the distinction of being the only known Victorian to be certified in death as an outlaw.

Word of the gunfight raced through Kelly Country. When the news reached one young lady she was devastated. A little over a month later she would blow kisses in court as Ned answered charges of murder and she would intrigue Kelly enthusiasts for generations. Who was she? Nobody knows for sure. But she's a key figure in the search for a missing piece in the Kelly story—the woman who Ned was said to have loved and maybe even married.

In films and books over the years, we have almost had to make her up, this Maid Marian to Ned's Robin Hood. In the

Kelly film starring Mick Jagger, Ned married his sweetheart in gaol a few days before his death. Later, Heath Ledger romanced Naomi Watts, a fictitious squatter's daughter in the 2004 feature film *Ned Kelly*. And in *True History of the Kelly Gang*, the award-winning writer Peter Carey created Mary Hearn as Ned's lover and the mother of his daughter.

The real Maid Marian, if there was one, is harder to find. There have been many claims over the years that Ned had secretly married, the first possibly made by Ned himself. A witness to a speech Ned made to his captives at Jerilderie claimed that Ned had said he had 'been only three weeks married' when he was outlawed in 1878. This random phrase stood alone like an island rock in a torrent of rhetoric and the witness who reported it may have been drunk at the time. On its own, the alleged comment does not make any sense. There are no records to indicate Ned ever married—but then there is no proof that he did not.

There have been stories, of course, including one in which he married the Jerilderie barmaid Mary Jordan, known as Mary the Larrikin. There is no evidence to back it up, and the records show that it was Joe, not Ned, who had enjoyed Mary's charms during the raid on Jerilderie. There must have been something about Mary, because she lives on in the story. But she wasn't Mrs Edward Kelly.

Ned has been romantically linked to several other women. The Kelly researcher Gary Dean suggests Ned might have married a barmaid known as 'Madela'. This claim was first made by Constable James Dwyer, who wrote in a police report that Madela had 'several times mentioned . . . having received a splendid watch from Ned Kelly'. Dwyer said the watch was 'certainly' the one stolen from Sergeant Kennedy. The police, however, do not seem to have taken this report seriously and appeared to doubt that Madela existed.

Ned has also been linked to the daughter of a sympathiser, Mary Miller, and to Aaron Sherritt's sister, Ann, while a churchman's wife later claimed her husband married Ned and his unnamed lover in New South Wales. Max Brown's 1948 biography of Ned Kelly, *Australian Son*, noted that family lore indicated Ned was romantically involved with Mary Miller. As Brown acknowledged, however, this was based on hearsay. Not surprisingly, the two best candidates for Maid Marian come from within the wider clan. The two women were Steve Hart's sister Esther (Ettie) and Ned's first cousin Kate Lloyd. Ettie Hart's great-great-grandson Paul O'Keefe said it has always been a family secret that Ettie was Ned's girlfriend. O'Keefe recently discovered a treasure trove of old family documents, including a scrapbook of poetry he believes might have been written by his great-great-grandmother. The melancholy love poems tell of 'blown kisses' to a vanished lover, and O'Keefe believes this was Ned. O'Keefe also believes the presence of Steve Hart in the Kelly Gang is a telling factor. He believes Steve was 'an accidental bushranger' and that he joined the gang mainly because he was the brother of Ned Kelly's girlfriend.

A romance between Ettie and Ned has gained some acceptance. It was supported by the history professor John Moloney in his 1980 book, *I am Ned Kelly*. In it, Moloney wrote that Ned and Ettie were deeply linked but their romance was severed by Ned's outlawry. After the siege, Ettie was hysterical with grief 'but no-one dared to ask whether she mourned for Steve alone or for the dark leader and loved one of days now gone'. After Ned's death, Ettie appeared in public with Kate Kelly in a short-lived stage production of the Kelly story. Ettie Hart married John Williams three years after Ned's execution and they had two children.

Ned's biographer Ian Jones, however, believes Kate Lloyd was Ned's true love. Kate was the only family member to meet Ned at the Benalla train station after his capture and a witness said the teenaged Kate 'cried without restraint'. And the Glenrowan publican's wife, Hanorah McDonnell, said: 'She will break her heart, poor girl, if he is hanged.' Adding weight to the case for Kate is a pictogram carved into the wooden stock of Ned's Snider-Enfield rifle. It used words and images to say, 'Dear Kate, you are in my heart.' The rifle is in the State Library collection in Melbourne.

Jones believes Kate was the young lady in the Beechworth courthouse. He says it is even possible they had a token marriage in gaol, the day before Ned's execution. Kate definitely visited Ned there and a priest was present. Ian Jones believes the priest, Dean O'Hea, could have conducted a 'personal sacrament between the two young people in this terrible place'. There are no records of a wedding taking place but as the marriage could not have been consummated it would not have been legitimate in the eyes of the church. For this reason, there would be no record of registration.

So, was Ned misheard when he supposedly said at Jerilderie that he had been married? Was he lying? Or could he have been referring to a betrothal of sorts to Kate or Ettie? We may never know, but if there was a romance between Ned and either of the two young women then it was doomed from the start. We do know that Ettie and Kate were devastated by the destruction of the gang, and even if neither was Ned's true love they were both among the saddest victims of the Last Stand.

17
ANATOMY OF A GUNFIGHT

'Fear and panic in the dark.'

The breakthroughs at the dig arrived quietly. In the final days, the bottom layers were scraped out of the western bedroom, the one in which the bodies of Dan and Steve were found. A search beneath the ashes of a charred sill beam revealed a small copper cap. Jon Sterenberg had to photograph it *in situ* before it could be lifted from the soil and identified but its depth and location meant that it was probably associated with the siege. Sterenberg, who had a good working knowledge of ballistics, already had an idea of what he was looking at.

A quick inspection found a crescent-shaped indent on the base. This was the mark left by a rifle hammer 128 years earlier, proving it was a percussion cap from a particularly old firearm. Because it was found inside the building it seemed to be the first evidence of return fire from the holed-up Kelly Gang. This was a significant discovery that could provide new evidence about the gang's activities during the siege. But who fired it and when? An examination of the weaponry used by the Kellys could find a link to the percussion cap and the man who fired it.

This tiny artefact was last held by Ned Kelly. Courtesy Reece Rayner and Neal Kelly.

When the outbreak began, the Kellys were lightly armed. By the time of the siege, they had amassed an impressive arsenal of rifles, shotguns and revolvers. After the killings at Stringybark Creek, the gang strengthened their armoury by making off with police weapons, including four Webley revolvers and the shotgun later used to murder Aaron Sherritt. A Martini-Henry rifle was added to the collection after it was dropped by a policeman near Greta one night. This was the rifle used to test the prototype of the armour. On the way to Euroa, Ned bailed up a hunting party and stole the Snider-Enfield rifle that he nicknamed 'Betty', possibly in tribute to the American frontiersman Davy Crockett and his Kentucky long rifle, 'Betsy'. The raids on Euroa and Jerilderie also netted at least half-a-dozen revolvers, some obsolete. Two rifles were legally purchased—a Winchester and a Colt revolver with an alarming tendency to backfire. With the gang's original weapons it brought the number of guns in the arsenal to about thirty.

Ned took the gun that he used at Stringybark Creek to Glenrowan. This was a battered old sawn-off carbine that Harry Power might have given him in their early days together. It was literally held together with string and said to have such a curve in the barrel that it could shoot around corners. Despite its shortcomings, Ned was attached to it and boasted of his prowess with it. At Stringybark Creek, he told the policeman McIntyre: 'I will back it against any gun in the country—I can shoot a kangaroo at 100 yards.'

The best of the weapons obtained by the gang were not used in the siege. The quality rifles, including 'Betty', were given to the sympathisers, probably for use in the uprising. The gang kept many of the revolvers—Ned had four—and at least one shotgun. He also had the antique carbine and the back-firing Colt.

The percussion cap could only be linked to a few weapons at the inn, namely the pistols and the Colt, because these were the ones that used the antiquated system of powder-filled caps to fire a ball. Now the question was whether the cap came from one of the pistols or Ned Kelly's alarmingly unreliable revolving rifle.

The answer lay in matching that rifle to the percussion cap. The Hammond family of Canberra owns the old Colt rifle as well as Joe Byrne's suit of armour. Both treasures have been handed down through the family since the police superintendent Francis Hare gave them to Rupert Hammond's ancestor, Sir William Clarke, soon after the siege. Hare had convalesced after his wrist injury at the Clarke family estate, 'Rupertswood', near Melbourne, and said he presented the family with the armour and rifle as a gesture of thanks.

These were princely gifts and Rupert Hammond is sceptical about Hare's real motives. Hammond thinks Hare was nervous about the looming Royal Commission and hoped to win favour from powerful people. Sir William was a member of parliament and would have been well placed to help the superintendent ride out the storm—but there is no evidence he did so.

As part of the filming of the Renegade Films television documentary *Ned Kelly Uncovered*, Rupert Hammond brought the old rifle to Glenrowan in November 2008. A retired Victoria Police comparative analysis expert, Henry Huggins, was brought in to compare the percussion cap with the weapon. He identified the cap as a 'top hat' type, larger than those used in pistols and therefore from a rifle. The first box was ticked; the pistols used in the siege could be ruled out.

Huggins fitted a makeshift foil cap over the firing nipple and dry-fired Rupert Hammond's rifle. Then he used a microscope to compare the hammer strike on the foil with the original strike mark on the percussion cap. The hammer on the Hammond rifle had a small deformity that left a divot on the foil cap. There was a matching divot on the old percussion cap. It confirmed that the ancient firearm owned by Rupert Hammond really was Ned Kelly's Colt revolving rifle. It seemed to show that Ned had been the last person to handle the percussion cap as he fought for his life 128 years earlier.

But the dig still had one more secret to reveal and this would help to reconstruct how the Kellys fought their battle as bullets raked the inn. The archaeologists had joked that the best discoveries are sometimes not made until a dig is almost over and it proved true on the second last day, when a small, flattened shell was found in the rear bedroom. It was a revolver cartridge that had been fired during the siege. Three more cartridges from the same weapon and a shotgun shell were found nearby. This was an exciting moment for Adam Ford because he thought the cache of cartridges could reveal something about the men who had discarded them.

Discarded spent cartridges illuminate frantic moments in the gunfight. Courtesy Reece Rayner and Neal Kelly.

A quick check of the inn's floor plan firmed up a rapidly forming theory. It showed that any bullets coming through the front of the inn would have hit the interior walls at the back of the bar, parlour and dining room. Importantly, molten remains of spent bullets that had earlier been discovered in a line at the foot of these interior walls indicated that some of those slugs either became lodged in the timber or fell to the floor. That meant the two bedrooms at the back offered some protection from the killing zone in the front rooms. And that knowledge helped Ford make a remarkable deduction about the conduct of the gunfight.

There were no windows at the eastern and western sides of the inn and the windows in the back walls of the bedrooms opened directly onto the breezeway between the inn and the Jones home. This meant that the gang had to venture into the bar, dining room or parlour to shoot at the police through the windows or doors, and the front rooms were very dangerous places, even in armour.

Reloading would have been a complicated process in the darkened front rooms and suicidal with a light. Because the bedroom windows opened onto the dark breezeway, however, a lantern could burn there without alerting the police and illuminating the gang as targets. It seemed the Kellys had bunkered down in the bedroom, desperately reloading and discarding the shells before braving the bullet-shredded front rooms to fire back at the advancing police. For Adam Ford, the discarded cartridges and the old shotgun shell dropped against the bed-room wall painted a vivid scene that would not have been out of place in a Western movie. 'So we've got two sides of the conflict,' he said:

> This is very evocative because it gives us a picture of these guys crouching and reloading behind the wall as the police attacked the front. This has added some extra powerful imagery. I'm really excited about this.

The historian Ian Jones had doubts that the scattered car-tridges proved the bedroom was safe from police fire. He pointed out that the police also attacked the western side of the building and while they could not have seen into the bedroom, its flimsy western wall would have offered little defence against bullets. Jones believed it was likely the outlaws did use the bedroom to reload, however, and he felt the percussion cap from Ned's rifle could be linked to the final conversation between Ned and Joe. When Ned asked his mate to load his rifle they were standing in the darkened breezeway. It was probably too dark there for the complicated process of fitting the caps to the rifle but if they moved into the lamp-lit bedroom the injured bushrangers could see well enough to reload for the next round. Jones believes this was when the used percussion cap from Ned's rifle was dropped—a powerful physical reminder of a remarkable moment in the siege.

There was not much to do on the final day of the dig. Some small jobs, mainly administrative, had to be completed before the excavator could move in and re-bury the remains of Ann Jones' inn. Archaeology by nature is a destructive process and the inn had now been scraped clean. It is unlikely anyone will excavate that part of the site again because finally, after more than a century of depredation, the inn has nothing left to give up. Ann's home and kitchen remain, of course, another story.

Before the piles of spoil were pushed back in there was a last chance to study the footprint of the inn. Even though the western parlour wall had been lost, the post holes helped the archaeologists produce a floor plan that matched the oral accounts of three rooms along the front and two bedrooms separated by a passage at the rear. The confused nature of the post holes made it difficult to define some of the inner walls but the archaeology and photographic records can be combined to show the dining room was probably the largest room. At about five metres wide by four deep, it was not much bigger than a large modern garden shed. The bar room in the centre was a little smaller and the parlour smaller still. Relaxing by the parlour fire would have been a very cosy affair. The rectangular bedrooms stretched at the rear of the house. With their windows opening onto a shaded breezeway, these rooms would have been cool and dimly lit but as the archaeology showed, they were decorated to make the visitor's stay a pleasant one.

The historian and nineteenth-century hotels expert Dr Clare Wright visited the site during the dig. She found the close confines of the inn revealing in both a historical and human sense. In our modern age, where we can communicate from half a world away without ever meeting, Wright saw the floor plan as a reminder of a time when people's lives were so closely entwined that they almost lived on top of each other. The hostage descendant and author Judith Douthie had a similar reaction; for her it helped to cement her understanding of the terrible hours of the siege. 'I can't believe more people weren't killed,' she said.

> There was such a concentration of people in such a small place and to have bullets whizzing around their ears, it was no wonder they were all crying and saying their prayers.

Lloyd-Hart descendant Noeleen Lloyd was pleased to have confirmation that there was no cellar beneath the pub. She hoped it would help to kill off the stories that Dan and Steve had survived. And, like her friend Judith Douthie, Noeleen Lloyd was struck by the close confines of the inn:

> When you see it all opened up you can see there was nowhere for anybody to hide in the pub, but one of the things that stunned me was just how small the hotel was and what it must have been like for so many people crammed into that little building.

Kelly family descendant Anthony Griffiths was not given to flights of fantasy about the siege or the people involved, and rather saw the dig as a valuable scientific and academic exercise that would help to decide the site's future. Still, an inspection of the cap and cartridges sent a little tingle down his spine:

> For Kelly buffs looking for a bigger story I don't think it added anything really but it did add something on an

academic level and I was expecting them to come up with a fair host of these little artefacts, because that was really what the archaeology was all about. But looking at the shell casings that were actually used in the siege, well, that was a little bit eerie.

It was a sentiment echoed in a report that Adam Ford produced two years after the dig was completed:

All of a sudden, the site was stripped of the legend and romanticism and in their place flashed images of fear and panic in the dark of a tiny-roomed, simple bush pub, of violence and the deaths of three young men. For them, this was not a heroic stand but a fight for their lives after a plan gone wrong.

The archaeology had served to add a strong human element to the story. The ballistics items told the story of the gunbattle and helped to provide a clearer picture of how four men—hopelessly outnumbered—fought to the death because there was nothing else they could do. The everyday items from the pub gave an insight into the life of a woman who simply wanted to make something for herself and failed. And it served up touching reminders that five people died here, including an innocent child and a curious old man.

18

AFTERMATH

'An illegal act for the sake of gain.'

In an archaeological sense, the post holes of the inn were among the most important discoveries but perhaps the most poignant were those left by the least significant and shortest-lived building that ever went up there. During the dig, these small holes had been a nuisance to the archaeologists and served only to confuse the understanding of the site. But they were also tangible evidence of the sad time when Ann Jones and her dwindling family huddled together in a freezing lean-to, with the ashes of their old life beneath their feet.

Ann came back to Glenrowan after the death of her son. For several months, Ann, the wounded Jane and the three surviving boys lived in the rough hut erected against the ruined parlour chimney. It was a hard life with little money, and for food and other basics Ann often had no choice but to rely on the generosity of her neighbours. It was a humbling position. During the siege at the 'House of Sport' she had enjoyed the sudden superiority she had found over her fellow Glenrowaners and seems to have offended several. The ill-feeling seemed particularly pronounced among the Reardons, while the bad blood between Ann and the Kelly supporters had worsened. Some of those she had treated so dismissively in the past now kept her family alive with donations of food and firewood through a bitter winter.

But then things got even worse. On 10 November—four months after the siege—Ann was arrested and charged with harbouring the outlaws. She was carted off to Melbourne, where she faced a police court and was promptly remanded to appear in Wangaratta on the twenty-seventh of that month. Bail was set at a staggering £600. Ann's lawyer, David Gaunson, (who later represented Ned Kelly at his murder trial) argued it down to £400. It made no difference to the penniless Ann and she spent a week in Melbourne Gaol awaiting her next court date.

Her committal hearing later that month was a humiliating experience during which her morals went on trial as much as her actions. A scapegoat was needed and Ann's behaviour during the siege made her an easy target. The court heard phrases such as 'endearments towards Ned', 'bit of a boss', and 'lends her daughter'. There was evidence of 'intimate' moments with Ned and Joe. In damning testimony, Ann's former friends and neighbours said she was a willing supporter of the Kellys during the siege. Looking 'pale and careworn' in the courtroom, she was depicted as something of a harlot; a woman who had aided and abetted the outlaws for her own selfish purposes.

The Age reported:

Mr. Chomley, the Crown Prosecutor, stated . . . she had not acted from motives of romance, sympathy, or love for

Kelly or his companions, but had committed an illegal act for the sake of gain.

There was no mention of what that gain might have been. Partly through circumstances and partly through her own poor decisions, Ann had gained nothing and lost almost everything. Now she was being singled out as the only person to face trial over the Glenrowan siege. The police and government might have hoped her prosecution would act as a circuit breaker for the anger among the settlers after the siege. If so, it served little purpose and when Ann went to trial at Beechworth in May the following year she was quickly acquitted. Now she was a free woman, but one who had suffered greatly, and she was even more distrusted by her community. Generations would pass before she got a fair go from the public. As Alex McDermott and Clare Wright wrote in the essay 'Ned's Women', there was precious little support for her at the time:

Ann Jones was stuck between a rock and a hard place. Hated by the selector sympathisers for being cosy with the police and pursued by the police for being an avaricious slut. No-one, it seems, entertained the idea that Ann was making the best of a bad lot, inspired by gun-wielding desperadoes to protect her children and her property through any available means.

Soon after her arrest, Ann had left the rough humpy behind and joined her husband in Gippsland. She stayed there with Owen for about nine months and later declared him to be the 'best husband there was'. Best husband or not, Ann eventually returned to the north-east (she said the cold, damp Gippsland weather was bad for her health) and she lived for a time with her eldest daughter near Wodonga before returning to Glenrowan, where she stayed for the rest of her life.

Back at home, Ann fought a long and determined campaign to get compensation for her personal and financial losses. She wrote to the authorities and collected signatures for a petition. She went to parliament and the press. She was seen in the streets of towns and villages, urging passersby to support her case. When a compensation board was set up she tried to get £500. The board refused to consider loss of life as a factor for compensation and awarded her £305 for her property losses, and later reduced that to just £265. Reporting on the claim, *The Argus* rather meanly noted that while Ann had been found not guilty of harbouring the outlaws, 'it is another [thing] to resolve that she is innocent and should be compensated'.

Jane Jones' health steadily deteriorated after the siege and in April 1882 she died of tuberculosis, aged seventeen. Ann always blamed Jane's death on the trauma of seeing her brother killed. Jane was buried at the Wangaratta cemetery but Ann could not afford to erect a fence around the grave. Ann continued to write to the police, politicians and the press and finally it paid off. She was awarded a further £100 for the death of her son, taking the total to £365. This was the monetary value set on the grief dealt to Ann Jones.

She put the money towards a new hotel on the site of the first one but in an act of petty vengeance the authorities refused to grant her a liquor licence, forcing her to lease the new building to the police. Owen Jones died in 1890 and in that year Ann married an Englishman, Henry Smith. Some time later Ann and Henry won a licence to sell wine and they ran their new hotel until 1901. Three years later it, too, burnt down. Henry—thirty years Ann's junior—died in the same year and, according to Ann, left her £2000—enough to live off the interest. Finally, she had some security but she had paid a high price for it.

Ann could have started a new life elsewhere but for some reason she decided to stay in Glenrowan. It was a decision that puzzled the journalist Brian Cookson thirty years later when he interviewed Ann as she neared death 'just a stone's throw away' from the site of the tragedy. Cookson visited Ann over two days at her gloomy cottage in Glenrowan. He told how the old woman coughed and choked as she railed against the police and the Kellys. Mostly, she mourned the deaths of her children. At the end, only five of the eleven children she had delivered were still alive; Margaret and her husband were in Deniliquin, New South Wales, while Owen, Jerry and Heddington were in Western Australia. Tom was 'a farmer somewhere in New South Wales'. Cookson left Ann in the dreary cottage 'with nothing of brightness' and only bitter memories for her final days.

> Exhausted with the strain of her narrative, the old woman lay back upon the pillow weeping bitterly. In a broken voice she bade her visitor farewell. 'I shall not be long here,' she moaned. 'Soon I shall see my dear murdered children again! Goodbye! God bless you for letting me shake the hand of an Englishman in this accursed place.'

Cookson finished his report linking the sad old woman of Glenrowan with another sad old woman who lived just a few miles away. Ann Jones and Ellen Kelly were both still grieving the events of June 1880. Ann died in 1910, soon after speaking to Cookson. She was buried at the Wangaratta cemetery, near Johnny and Jane. Ellen Kelly lived long enough to be photographed in a motorcar and gained the respect and dignity denied to her in her earlier life, but she, too, carried scars for all of her long life. Ellen died in 1923 and she was laid to rest near two of her children at Greta.

For some families, the bitterness lasted for generations. Most of the hostages made full recoveries but a few carried mental and physical injuries for life. For some of the others at the siege, life was cut short.

The honest policeman Hugh Bracken was one of the victims. After the siege, he received £275 of the Kelly reward money (in fact he applied for £4000) and it was too dangerous for him to remain in the north-east. He was transferred to Richmond in Melbourne, where he did not get a warm welcome from some of his police colleagues, who resented him for preventing Sergeant Steele from killing Ned Kelly. In 1883, Bracken had a breakdown and his wife died the following year. When he recovered, he soldiered on as a single father to his sons and married again. In 1900, he shot himself at his home near Wallan. He was fifty-nine.

Thomas Curnow's life was in mortal danger for every moment he remained in Kelly Country. His schoolhouse was immediately closed and he was quickly transferred to Melbourne and then to Ballarat, where he took a pay cut to teach at a new school. His wife, Jean, always lived in fear that the Kelly supporters would get their vengeance. Curnow's descendant Judith Douthie said Thomas was occasionally threatened after the siege. Once, as he walked through a park in Ballarat, a man shouted from behind, 'We'll get you, Curnow!' Thomas pretended not to hear and walked on.

In 1911, Cookson wrote of Curnow's latter years teaching under an assumed name at a small school in the 'wilderness of Gippsland'. The reference to Gippsland might have been a smokescreen to hide the fact that Thomas was really living in Ballarat. Cookson said Thomas' secret was known to some 'but they respect his wishes by seldom or never alluding to it'. The reporter found a man with no regrets.

> And so, in the placid serenity of his autumn of life, Mr Curnow goes on with the work that he has always followed; the instruction of the young. And a wise and capable instructor he has proved himself.

For his bravery—or his treachery—Thomas was awarded £550 of the Kelly reward money. He later said money was never his motivation for stopping the train, but appealed for more anyway. He pointed out that his family had suffered financially from the forced move. He was awarded another £450 and a handsome mantle clock, making him the recipient of the largest reward. When he died in 1922, Thomas was buried at the old Ballarat cemetery near his parents. His headstone was inscribed with the alias 'Ginge' Curnow in the hope that his grave would not be desecrated.

Life went on after the siege and the hostages faded from public view but some, like the teenaged Thomas Cameron, left valuable accounts for future generations. Thomas's letter to his brother gave evidence of the mayhem when bullets whizzed by, breaking the clock and smashing the furniture. A passage ended with a damning indictment of the police: 'And the worst of it was that they knew we were in there.' Thomas Cameron grew up to become a successful businessman in central-western New South Wales and had six children. He died in 1937 at the age of seventy-three.

John Delaney—who had been so frightened by Ned Kelly that he had crushed his pipestem between his teeth—gave evidence at Ann's trial. He described her as 'a bit of a boss'. John died in 1910. Jack McHugh—who had so bravely tried to save Johnny Jones under gunfire—received no reward. He remained in the north-east until his death nineteen years later. The gravel carter John Lowe did a service to history when he wrote down his memories of the siege eleven years before his death in 1950. A football oval in the border town of Yarrawonga was named after him. Lowe's boss, the gravel contractor Alfonso Piazzi, died in 1881. Piazzi's tent-mate, the 'strange woman from Benalla', remains a mystery. It was almost as if she had never been there. Her name is not known and her appearance goes down as a cameo, albeit an entertaining one.

David Mortimer had seven children and lived to old age. He is best known for playing the concertina at the 'House of Sport' and he always kept his love of music and enjoyed playing the fiddle for his family. Unlike some of the hostages, David was happy to speak about the siege to his loved ones, although the memory of Johnny Jones' dying screams never left him. In 1944, Albury-Wodonga's *Border Morning Mail* interviewed David for an article headed 'I was at the Kelly Gang Roundup'—the inspiration for Judith Douthie's book. In the report, Mortimer said the 'bushrangers treated us quite well' and told of sharing a whiskey with Joe Byrne. David died in 1951.

The Reardons all survived the siege but nineteen-year-old Michael carried a shotgun slug in his shoulder all his life. Descendants of the Reardons still live in the north-east. Old family members say Michael never spoke of the siege. The railwayman Dennis Sullivan, who helped James Reardon remove the rail line, lived in the Euroa area and had some alcohol-related troubles with the law. He died in 1908. The stationmaster John Stanistreet and his family also moved away after the siege, when John was given a promotion to Gippsland. He died in 1896; his wife, Emily, outlived him by more than thirty years.

The policeman Francis Hare had harboured dreams of becoming commissioner but after the siege he made some ill-advised criticisms of his colleague Charles Nicolson, which did not help Hare's cause. Hare became a police magistrate in Melbourne. Later he went to work at the Clarkes' stately property 'Rupertswood', where he wrote his memoir of the Kelly years. He died at Rupertswood in July 1892. Nicolson became a judge and died in Melbourne in 1898. The controversial Sergeant Steele was awarded £290 of the Kelly reward money and remained a policeman in Wangaratta, where he was held in high regard by the community. Steele seized Ned Kelly's blood-stained cartridge bag at the end of the Last Stand and showed it to Brian Cookson four years before his death in 1914.

The Aboriginal troopers who had so greatly alarmed Ned Kelly worked bravely for the police. The troopers were awarded £50 each for their efforts before and during the siege but they saw none of it; it was paid to the Queensland and Victorian governments because the Kelly Reward Board saw little point in giving money to 'persons unable to use it'. These young men from Queensland had names that perhaps reflected their country or their spirits or their ancestry but to the police—with the casual racism of the time—they were known as Hero, Jimmy, Johnny, Jacky, Sambo, Barney, Moses and Spider. Although they missed out on the reward money, the troopers were presented with breastplates commemorating their service.

Kate Kelly, a girl of 'uncommon beauty', captured the public imagination with her daring exploits during the outbreak. Five years after Ned's death she moved to Forbes in New South Wales, where she married William 'Bricky' Foster and they had six children. Kate went missing on 5 October 1898 and her body was found nine days later in the Lachlan River. In November, Jim Kelly went to Forbes and brought Kate's children back to Greta. Jim spent the rest of his life helping his mother care for the children.

After the Fitzpatrick Incident, Ned's sister Maggie Skillian separated from her husband and began a relationship with Tom Lloyd which lasted for the rest of Maggie's life. They had eleven children and named the eldest Edward, or Ned. After Maggie's death in 1896, Tom married Steve Hart's sister Rachel. Tom Lloyd, 'the fifth Kelly', died in 1927 and was buried at Greta. Unlike many of the others involved in the outbreak, Tom's grave was marked with a headstone.

History records that the siege took five lives—Johnny Jones, Martin Cherry and the three bushrangers, Dan, Steve and Joe. But there was a fatal postscript with the death of George Metcalf, who had been hit in the eyes while trying to shelter behind a chimney. Piazzi later told the police that Ned Kelly accidentally shot Metcalf when a pistol discharged by mistake but Metcalf always maintained it was a police bullet that struck the chimney. The police paid for his treatment in hospital.

As recounted by Judith Douthie, George was sent to Melbourne to recover. While there, he wrote to his sister, saying his wounded eyes were weak but 'getting on well'. In the letter, George also noted a curious description of a man he was lodging with, a gentleman with 'pink hair, green eyes, mauve eyebrows, swallowtail trousers and double barrelled frock coat with a tripe collar'. This eccentric chap must have been quite a sight, even for the vision-impaired George Metcalf. Soon after writing the letter, Metcalf took a turn for the worse and died from his injuries in October 1880.

The McAuliffe brothers were arrested when the last of the hostages were released from the inn. The brothers were detained for a short time but then let go without charge. The publicans Paddy and Hanorah McDonnell remained fervent sympathisers. After Ned's arrest, Mrs McDonnell made her feelings clear when she said she hoped Ned would not be hanged. Neither of the McDonnells was charged and they continued to run their pub in Glenrowan until it closed around the turn of the century. Their son Eugene then lived in the old pub and local old-timers remember him sitting on the front verandah and watching the world pass by.

After helping the gang put on their armour, the sympathiser James Kershaw took cover and survived the siege. He was not arrested. Never married, Kershaw lived in Greta for the rest of his life. Some of the sympathisers who were gathered outside the inn had committed offences that could have put them in prison for a long time but they also escaped retribution. Many of their descendants, including the Lloyd family, still live in Kelly Country.

People got on with life as best they could, although there were fractures in the community for several generations. Nationally, the Kelly story remained a sensation but in the district the siege was rarely discussed between locals and almost never with outsiders. Children were told not to ask about it and many people simply tried to pretend it had not happened. There were good reasons for this. One was self-preservation; after all, many of those involved were considered to be criminals. Another was simple neighbourly decency. People were devastated by grief and stigma. It just was not done to remind your friends and neighbours about the tragedies that had befallen their families. As with most small country communities, ties were close, friends were held dear, and a wrong word could cause pain. Partly for these reasons, little effort was made to hold on to the Glenrowan that Ned Kelly knew.

If Ned could see Beechworth now he would find plenty of familiar sights. Even in bustling Melbourne he might glimpse remnants of 1880 hidden in the forest of glass and steel. Tiny Glenrowan, though, would be almost unrecognisable to him. Apart from the railway platform, none of the buildings that were standing in 1880 have survived in their original locations and few people mourned the passing of a streetscape that reminded them of the troubles. When the wine shanty on the siege site became the Last Stand Café in the 1940s there was some discontent. Late one night somebody pulled down the sign at the front and it did not go back up. But time heals wounds, and it has now mended most of those inflicted during the Kelly years.

19

TRIAL AND RETRIBUTION

'Never mind, Ned, they are a lot of curs.'

The first stages of the Old Melbourne Gaol were built from 1841 and it housed some of Victoria's worst criminals until its closure in the 1920s. It had a brief renaissance as a prison during World War II but much of the original prison was demolished. One wing survives as a testament to a crueller time. It is a place of iron and stone. Rows of tiny cells sit upon each other like the chambers of an ants' nest and the only natural light filters through an arch high in the roof. Footfalls echo from the chilly walls. It is cold and gloomy and bleak—and that is just the way the tourists like it. Thousands visit each year and many come because of Ned Kelly.

Ned was taken there after the siege to be patched up in the prison hospital. From the moment he arrived, it was clear his imprisonment would be both physical and emotional because he would spend most of it isolated from his loved ones. Initially, Ned was not allowed contact with anyone but his gaolers. His mother Ellen was working in the women's section but she was kept from him until the next day, when the prison governor, John Castieau—a compassionate man—allowed a short meeting between mother and son. The reunion inside the bleak prison walls must have been bittersweet. To meet now at the end of things, in this grim place, was heartbreaking but it was also a moment to treasure—Ned would be allowed precious few meetings with his loved ones.

His sisters, Maggie, Kate and fourteen-year-old Grace—with Tom Lloyd—had travelled to Melbourne in a desperate attempt to see him. They were denied. It was unfair but the authorities said visitors might help Ned to take his own life. In the community, there was widespread grief and sympathy for Ned, expressed in letters he probably never received. One came from an anonymous friend and was sent from Ballarat. The State Library of Victoria holds the original.

Dear Ned,

I write a few lines to you hoping that you are not suffering pain now. I would like to see you dear Ned very much but it is no use in asking because they would not let your sisters see you. Even I do not give my name because the police would take me up for a sympathiser and I would not like that because I was never in Gaol before in my life. It is a nasty thing of [the Premier] Mr Berry not to let your sisters see you it is him that is doing it. I will say goodbye to you dear Ned and may god bless you. I hope if the police open this that they will give it to you. They might let me see you because I could do no harm. From a friend.

Intimidated by the police and frightened of retribution, the writer was nonetheless both saddened and outraged by the treatment handed to Ned. It was a small part of a wave of discontent among the poor. Ned was still at the head of this wave. He had been brought down but his cause had not. At the centre of a political and media storm, he would get political 'justice'— swift, decisive and not entirely fair.

His committal hearing was set for Monday 2 August. It was scheduled for the city court in Melbourne but over the weekend it was secretly switched to Beechworth for Friday 6 August, probably to prevent hordes of sympathisers crowding the courthouse. And so, on the morning of Sunday 1 August, Ned was taken by cab from the gaol to the train station. In *Ned Kelly's Last Days*, Alex and Jennifer Castles recorded that Ned had recovered enough to share a lighthearted moment with the prison governor, Castieau, who told Ned as he boarded the cab: 'Now, Kelly, your best game is to be quiet.'

Ned retorted: 'Damn it, ain't I always quiet?'

His mood fell as the train chugged north for his last trip to Kelly Country. Soon after they left Melbourne, Ned could see his beloved alpine ranges to the east. He is recorded as saying: 'There they are. Will I ever see them again?' He did see them once more, but only from the train window on the return trip to Melbourne. The train rolled through Euroa—the scene of one of Ned's greatest triumphs—and then to Glenrowan—the scene of his demise. The ruins of Ann's hotel could be seen from the windows on the left of the train carriage. Ned grew withdrawn and remarked: 'A good man fell there.' His police guards included the erratic Sergeant Steele. It must have given grim satisfaction to the police to hear Ned's lament for Joe as the charred remains of the inn slid by and the train rumbled over the newly repaired high point in the railway line just out of town.

The clandestine court switch did not remain a secret for long. By the time the train arrived at Beechworth, a huge crowd had gathered at the station. Some were supporters, others were simply eager to catch sight of the colony's most notorious man. The town's local paper, *The Ovens and Murray Advertiser*, noted that *sub judice* laws were in force and it had to restrain itself from convicting Ned before he faced court. The newspaper had previously described him as 'a notorious ruffian', a 'young desperado' and a man who 'wound up a whole life of thieving by a series of deliberate and dastardly murders'. Now it settled for referring to him as a 'notorious bushranger and murderer' but otherwise promised to temper its remarks, at least until the legal proceedings were finished. There had never been any question about how the *Advertiser* viewed Ned and doubtless it was hoping the courts would share the same opinion.

The Beechworth courthouse still stands and visitors can sit in the dock where Ned heard the case against him. He was charged with the murders of the policemen Lonigan and Scanlan—capital offences that would mean death if the verdict was guilty. The only option was to plead self-defence. Perhaps with that aim in mind, the family had engaged a Beechworth lawyer and member of the Opposition, William Zincke, who had earlier proved his worth in defending other members of the Greta Mob. Almost as an afterthought, the family decided a week later that another lawyer, who was also a member of parliament, would be a useful addition to the defence team. Tom and Maggie then engaged David Gaunson, who was a Melbourne solicitor and also the member for Ararat, to help with the fight for Ned's life. But Zincke refused to work with Gaunson and promptly resigned from the case. Gaunson was now the sole member of the defence.

The courtroom was soon full and crowds of people thronged outside, desperate to hear whether Ned would go on trial for his life. The *Advertiser* noted rather disapprovingly that the 'gallery was inconveniently crowded with members of the softer sex'. The women included Ned's sister Maggie but one young lady in particular attracted the interest of observers. *The Illustrated Australian News* reported that many sympathisers were present, 'especially among the ladies [but] one young girl of good looks and respectable attire showed questionable taste in going to the extent of kissing hands to the outlaw'. Apparently moved by this gesture, Ned 'returned the compliment with interest'. Later, the author of a letter to the editor of the *Advertiser* sniffed: 'Whoever heard of any prisoner on trial for his life being permitted to wave his handkerchief in the dock, and kiss his hand to his sweetheart?' Sadly, none of the reporters thought to ask who she was.

Gaunson's motives for defending Ned have been the subject of debate. It has been suggested he was more interested in furthering his career than fighting for the underdog. Nevertheless, he threw himself into the defence of his infamous client. On the morning of the first day, he mounted a scarifying attack on the decision to isolate Ned from his loved ones. It was nonsense, he said, to claim it was dangerous to let friends and relatives see Ned. 'To deny him that right is a monstrous tyranny and I should fail in my duty if I did not denounce it,' Gaunson thundered. The lawyer had nailed the heart of the matter; it was actually a fight against monstrous tyranny that had led to this courtroom. But David Gaunson was hopelessly underprepared for the case. He was so new to it that his preparation consisted only of catching up on back copies of newspapers. He sought an adjournment to do some more research and it was reluctantly granted.

As the court rose, *The Argus* reporter witnessed a moving exchange between Ned and his sister Maggie. 'Before Kelly could be removed from the dock, Mrs (Maggie) Skillian and Tom Lloyd stepped forward and shook hands with him,' said *The Argus*.

He [Ned] remarked to Mrs Skillian, 'It looks as if they won't let me see you—good bye.' Mrs Skillian replied, 'Never mind, Ned, they are a lot of curs,' to which the prisoner rejoined, 'there's one native that's no cur, and he will show them that yet'.

Ned's defiance was unabated. He would need all the self-belief he could muster because his committal hearing was all but a foregone conclusion and his trial would be without hope.

The court took evidence over three days. Among others, it heard from McIntyre, the policeman who had fled at Stringybark Creek and hidden in a wombat hole, as well as Senior Constable John Kelly and Robert Scott of the bank at Euroa. Ned said nothing in his defence but Gaunson handed out a courtroom savaging to prosecution witnesses, especially McIntyre. It did no good, and at the end Ned Kelly was ordered to stand trial for murder.

Ned Kelly's sister Maggie Skillian. Photographer D Ilsley. Image courtesy of the Pictures Collection, State Library of Victoria.

The trial was to be held in Melbourne. This would do nicely for those who did not wish to see Ned judged by a jury of country folk. Even worse for the Kellys, they soon learned that the judge who would hear Ned's trial was none other than Sir Redmond Barry, the man who had sent Ellen Kelly to prison in 1878.

Today, a statue of Barry stands outside the State Library in Melbourne. Kelly supporters take delight in the fact that pigeons defecate on his head. It is a rather childish vengeance but they find it satisfying nonetheless. The fastidious Irishman was regarded as a scourge of the lower class and given to harsh judgements, even by the standards of his time.

Redmond Barry took a hard line on bushrangers. Thirteen years earlier he had ordered a flogging for a teenager who had tried and failed to rob three men near Melbourne. The judge felt fifteen-year-old William Parsons would have benefitted had he already undergone the 'correction of the rod'. Luckily for young Parsons, the lashing could not be carried out until he was sixteen and by then flogging was no longer legal. It was, however, typical of Barry's attitude to criminals; he was a 'hanging judge', who had sentenced Ned's uncle James to death for arson in 1868. The excessive severity of the penalty was shown up when the sentence was reduced to fifteen years in prison. And when Ellen Kelly went to trial for the attack on Fitzpatrick, Barry overlooked the weaknesses of Fitzpatrick's evidence and sentenced her to three years. He handed out six years each to the Kelly friends Skillian and Williamson.

Thus, the judge's track record did not inspire hope for Ned's supporters. Nevertheless, they hurled themselves into organising a defence. The trouble was, this would cost a lot of money and they had very little.

It was rumoured the gang had hidden loot from its bank raids, perhaps sparked by the fact that some of the money shared out after the robberies was stained with soil, apparently having been buried for a time. Fantasies persist today that the Kellys' bandit treasures are still hidden away in the hills. The reality is that the robberies—although lucrative—netted relatively small amounts compared to some of the spectacular hauls brought in by bushrangers in years gone by. The loot was quickly spent or divided soon after the robberies and if there was any hidden away, it was not found for the trial.

Since the Fitzpatrick Incident, with her husband and mother in gaol, Maggie Skillian had been caring for four of Ellen's children. The youngest, the infant Alice, was in gaol with Ellen. During this time, Maggie had also played a dramatic role in the outbreak. With her sister Kate, she had led sensational horse rides to meet and resupply her outlawed brothers under the noses of the police. Now she and Tom Lloyd were working together frantically to raise money to save Ned from the rope. They collected some from their friends but not enough. When Maggie went to mortgage her mother's selection to get a loan, she discovered that the authorities were playing dirty. The government blocked the loan at the request of the police. Whatever Ned had done, this would not be a fair fight.

The family had engaged a Melbourne barrister named Molesworth but he pulled out when it became apparent his fee would not be met. Then it got even worse, when Gaunson—who was not a barrister and could not appear in the Supreme Court—hired thirty-seven-year-old Henry Bindon to represent Ned at trial. Bindon had been a barrister for less than a year and had been in England for most of the Kelly outbreak. He knew very little about the case but now he was fighting for Ned's life.

Gaunson might have hoped the appointment of the inexperienced Bindon would force the judge to agree to an adjournment, thus allowing more time to raise money for the defence, but, if so, it backfired. Barry was determined to hear the trial immediately and he hoped to wrap it up in just one day. So keen was the judge to deliver quick justice to Ned that he had gas lighting fitted to the courtroom so the case could continue late into the night if need be. In the end, it took two days.

On the morning of 28 October, Ned went on trial for his life, represented by an inexperienced barrister who did not understand his case before a judge who had probably already made up his mind. A huge crowd gathered in the gallery and outside the court. Inside, the jury heard evidence from the policemen McIntyre and Kelly. Two of Ned's victims, the Jerilderie bank manager, John Tarleton, and the Euroa bank manager, Robert Scott, also testified. Perhaps unexpectedly, they somewhat bolstered the defence case; Tarleton by repeating Ned's claims he had shot the police at Stringybark Creek in self-defence; and Scott, by pointing out Ned's chivalrous treatment of the bank manager's finely dressed wife. McIntyre's evidence, which had changed since his first account of the shootings, was devastating. After initially saying that Lonigan had been shot while reaching for his pistol, McIntyre now told the court that Ned had killed Lonigan in cold blood.

Maggie Skillian and Ned's cousins Kate and Tom Lloyd gathered in the courtroom. In a tactical error, Bindon succeeded in blocking the use of the Jerilderie Letter for the prosecution. It meant the letter, with its strident claims of self-defence, could not be used as evidence for Ned. It sat on a table at the bar unread, denying Ned the opportunity of claiming the moral legitimacy, at least, of a rebel rather than a criminal.

Bindon stumbled further. He offered no witnesses in defence. Both sides then summed up and the judge gave a biased direction to the jurors, saying they must either convict Ned of murder or acquit him. Manslaughter was not an option. Even if Ned had been able to argue he had killed the police in self-defence, the jury was all but ordered to reject it. At the end of the second day, the jurors retired for just half an hour and came back with a verdict. Ned Kelly was guilty of murdering Thomas Lonigan.

Finally, too late, Ned addressed the court. He blamed himself for his flimsy defence and wished that he had spoken up in court. He said he feared death 'as little as to drink a cup of tea' but he regretted the lost opportunity to have his say.

'I lay blame on myself that I did not get up yesterday and examine the witnesses but I thought, if I did so, it would look like bravado and flashness and people might have said that I thought myself cleverer than Counsel. So I let it go as it was,' he said.

Redmond Barry was unimpressed. He placed the traditional black square of cloth on his head for his final exchange with Ned. What followed was a spirited and compelling conversation between the learned man of the law, and the charismatic but poorly educated man outside of the law. Barry had the black square and the power to dispense death but history gives the moral victory to Ned. He protested his innocence and even correctly argued a point of law with the learned judge. Barry stated that Ned had stolen 200 horses, to which Ned replied: 'Who proves that?' It was a simple question but one that cut straight to the bedrock of English law—an accused man is presumed innocent until proven guilty.

But the judge was inclined to overlook several hundred years of legal tradition. He replied that Ned was 'self-accused', having freely admitted to the horse thefts. It was true enough. Ned had stolen the horses, and had said so himself. But he had noted that while he had been convicted of receiving, he was never found guilty of horse theft. So, in a technical sense, he was quite correct in his exchange with the judge. Not that it made any difference in the end—but it did say much about Barry's attitude towards the dispensation of justice when it came to Ned Kelly.

At the end, hanging judge Barry lived up to his reputation and pronounced: 'You will be taken from here to the place from whence you came, and thence . . . to a place of execution, and there you will be hanged by the neck until you be dead.' He finished his address with: 'May the Lord have mercy on your soul.'

Ned retorted: 'I will go a little further than that and say I will see you there, where I go.'

Ned's life might have been forfeit but on his final public stage, he had had the last word. Sir Redmond Barry died of complications from diabetes on the 23 November, just twelve days after Ned's execution. Surely Ned would have enjoyed the irony, if in fact he did see the judge 'there, where I go'.

Interestingly, at the same time as the dig in Glenrowan, Ned's trial was play-acted as part of a Law Week activity in Melbourne. An actor went on trial under modern terrorism laws. Ned's defence was led by the barristers Gerry Nash and Rob Stary, who in real life have acted for the underworld figures Tony Mokbel and Carl Williams. A Victorian Supreme Court judge, Justice Lex Lasry, presided in the role of Redmond Barry. The prosecutor was the former head of the National Crime Authority, Peter Faris QC. Playing up to his pretend role, Faris thundered (with tongue in cheek) that Ned was 'nothing more than an Irish Catholic secessionist dog'. But at the end of the trial the audience cheered: Ned had been found not guilty.

After the verdict, Ned was taken back to the gaol, where he would live out his days in the condemned cell. William Gaunson, the brother of Ned's solicitor, David, met with the premier, Graham Berry, and pleaded for Ned to be allowed to see his loved ones. Berry agreed to allow Ned to have visitors and on 30 October, Maggie, Tom and Kate Lloyd and two other friends were allowed to see Ned in the gaol. Later that day, he was again allowed to talk to his mother, through the bars of the cell.

But tens of thousands of supporters would not let Ned die without a fight. There were rallies in halls and hotels across Melbourne, and Gaunson organised a petition for clemency. It quickly gathered more than 30,000 signatures. A massive protest march was organised to demand mercy from the governor. Up north, in Kelly Country, there were clashes between pro- and anti-Kelly mobs. But the ears of the ruling classes were closed.

On Monday 3 November the Executive Council considered the petition and saw no reason to overturn Barry's death sentence, perhaps not surprising as the judge was a member of the council. The execution would go ahead on 11 November, just thirteen days after the guilty verdict. Gaunson organised a public meeting for the Friday night after the Executive Council decision. Thousands of people gathered in and around the Hippodrome in Exhibition Street, for a march on Government House. The Melbourne newspapers felt these protesters were among the worst people in society and hinted darkly that ladies of the night were among them. Beechworth's *The Ovens and Murray Advertiser* went further.

It will not be known to persons judging from a distance that the crowds of apparent sympathisers who were brought together by Mr Gaunson . . . were composed of the lowest portion of the population of a city which has, as its substratum, as villainous a class of blackguards and prostitutes as are to be found on the face of the earth.

There may well have been plenty of blackguards and prostitutes in the seething crowd, but the *Advertiser* was missing the point. It was precisely because this 'lowest portion' wanted a fair go that they were rallying behind Ned. At the meeting, Gaunson announced the protest march had been called off but he would instead lead a deputation to the governor the next day. The governor rebuffed the delegation and Gaunson promptly abandoned the campaign to save Ned. He never saw his client again.

During this time, Ned had remained defiant, singing 'secular' songs in his cell and warning that 40,000 police would be needed to contain the Kelly movement. In the days after his conviction, he wrote a series of letters to the governor. The Governor Letters were the last he would write. They had none of the strident authority of the Jerilderie and Cameron letters and lacked even the childish pathos of the 'black snake' note ten years earlier to James Babington. In fact, they were to a large degree self-serving. In these last letters, he claimed that he had never intended to wreck the train and intended only to take the police hostage in return for the release from gaol of his mother and friends. In a letter dated 5 November, Ned wrote:

My intention was to have the stationmaster to flash the danger light on the platform so as to stop the train, and he was to tell the Police to leave their firearms and horses in the train and walk out with their hands over their heads, and their lives would be spared.

In other letters, he said he intended a civilian (presumably Curnow) to claim the reward for the gang. He again denied he had murdered the police at Stringybark Creek, falsely claimed the police fired the first shots in the siege ('neither me nor my companions fired a single shot until after I was wounded') and that he and the gang tried to save the hostages from the police bullets by barricading the insides of the hotel walls. Right until the end, Ned was fighting to clear his name.

In his final letter, written from the condemned cell on the day before his death, he asked:

There is one wish, in conclusion, I would like you to grant me, that is the release of my mother before my execution, as detaining her in prison could not make any difference to the government now, for the day will come when all men are judged by their mercy and their deeds; and also if you would grant permission for my friends to have my body that they might bury it in consecrated ground.

The governor refused.

On 10 November, Ned posed against the bluestone walls of the prison for his last photograph. He is in leg irons but stands tall against the wall, with his crippled hands held in front. His hair is carefully coiffed and his full beard cascades down his chest. Ned was terribly wounded in a physical sense—the damage to his limbs was catastrophic and his body still carried toxic lead slugs—but in this final study we can still see power and presence in his stance. The image is reminiscent of the photograph taken at Beechworth some six years earlier, when he was proclaimed the north-east's heavyweight boxing champion. In this last photo, he is hours away from death but seems defiant to the end.

That afternoon, he was allowed a final meeting with his mother. It is said that they parted with a proud but enigmatic farewell from Ellen: 'I mind you'll die like a Kelly, son.' She never saw him again. Jim and Kate and young Grace—who would go on to leave a legacy of Kelly descendants across the north-east—also said their farewells at a poignant prison meeting. Ned was then allowed one last meeting with Kate and Tom Lloyd. He loved both dearly and it, too, must have been a painful parting.

That night, Ned slept poorly, awoke early the next morning and prayed and sang quietly to himself. Shortly before ten o'clock on 11 November, he was led from the old section of the gaol across a courtyard to the new wing which housed the gallows. As he crossed the courtyard, he commented on bunches of pretty flowers growing in the prison grounds. From there, he was led to a cell adjacent to the scaffold for his appointment with the hangman.

The executioner was an unpleasant-looking Briton named Elijah Upjohn. He had been transported to Van Diemen's Land for stealing shoes at the age of sixteen in 1838 and had rarely been far from trouble since. After his release, he became a carter and nightman in Ballarat and was convicted of carting night soil without a licence. When he was caught stealing some roosters, he was sent to Pentridge, where he volunteered to become the flagellator and hangman. With a 'hideous and carbuncled' face, Upjohn was described as having the perfect visage for a hangman.

Ned was to be Upjohn's first execution.

Ned was given the last sacraments by Charles O'Hea, the Catholic priest who had baptised him as an infant. Then Ned's arms were pinned behind his back and he was led from the condemned cell to the scaffold. The noose was placed around his neck, Ned even moving his head slightly to make Upjohn's job easier. Present were Doctor Barker, the prison governor, John Castieau, guards and members of the press. The newspapers gave us the words that are forever regarded as Ned's last.

'Such is life.'

Some believe it is more likely that Ned had uttered these immortal words when he was first told of the precise time for his execution. They are remembered as his final words before the gallows trapdoor snapped open, but in fact his last words might simply have been, 'Ah well, so it has come to this.' This final statement might even have been cut short by the rope: 'Ah well, so it has—'

Whatever was really said, the fatalistic and courageous 'Such is life' has become synonymous with Ned and everything he stood for. And so, this statement will always be as much a part of the Kelly mythology as the famous armour. A towering figure such as Ned Kelly deserves a stirring final statement and if he had not said these words, or something like them, we would have had to make them up.

A white cap was pulled over Ned's face and, on the stroke of ten, Upjohn pulled the lever that sent Ned Kelly crashing into eternity.

Perhaps with some satisfaction, the *Advertiser* reported: 'The body fell about eight feet and was brought up with a terrible jerk; Kelly being a large, heavy man. Death must have been instantaneous.'

A hush fell across the city as the clocks chimed ten and inside the prison a moan went up among the convicts in their gloomy cells. Half an hour later, Ned's body was taken down, beheaded and disembowelled. A death mask was made of his face and his torso was buried in an unconsecrated grave within the prison grounds. Ned Kelly was dead but instantly immortalised. He was only twenty-five. And that is how he remains to us today, a young man, undeniably brave and loyal, perhaps a murderer, perhaps a freedom fighter, certainly a thief, but also a champion of the poor. He was a man who respected women and liked children but also one who took three lives in the pursuit of fairness and justice in a savage society. A man both adored and reviled—in life and death he became a legend, and although he paid the ultimate price, his struggle had not been in vain.

Ned had made a statement to Gaunson during his committal hearing in Beechworth and the lawyer gave it to the press after the execution. These words would help to shape Ned's legacy. He had spent his bushranging career proclaiming his innocence of murder and justifying his reasons for taking up arms against his oppressors. It would please him to know that his words to Gaunson live on. The statement started with this:

> I do not pretend that I have led a blameless life, or that one fault justified another, but the public judging a case like mine should remember, that the darkest life may have a bright side, and that after the worst has been said against a man, he may, if he is heard, tell a story in his own rough way, that will perhaps lead them to [soften] the harshness of their thoughts against him, and find as many excuses for him as he would plead for himself.

It finished with an expression of hope that would be answered within just a generation or two.

> If my lips teach the public that men are made mad by bad treatment, and if the police are taught that they may not exasperate to madness men they persecute and ill-treat, my life will not be entirely thrown away. People who live in large towns have no idea of the tyrannical conduct of the police in the country places, far removed from court; they have no idea of the harsh and overbearing manner, in which they execute their duty, or how they neglect their duty and abuse their powers.
>
> Edward Kelly

Ned Kelly's butchered torso, minus the skull, remained in its prison grave for almost fifty years. In 1929, the remains, and those of other executed criminals, were exhumed to allow for the construction of the Working Men's College (now the Royal Melbourne Institute of Technology) on the prison grounds. At that time, students might have souvenired some of the remains, including teeth and bones. It was believed that the rest of the bones, including Ned's, were re-interred in unmarked graves at Pentridge prison in Melbourne's north.

In the years following the execution, Ned's skull went on display in a glass case at the gaol. In 1978, it was stolen. Later, a Western Australian man claimed to have the skull and in 2009, on the anniversary of Ned's execution, the man, a farmer named Tom Baxter, gave the skull to the Victorian Institute of Forensic Medicine for testing. In the same year, the remains of thirty-four executed criminals were exhumed from Pentridge and carefully sorted and tested. DNA was taken from the skeleton believed to be Ned's and compared with that of the Kelly descendant Leigh Olver. The result created headlines around the world. After 130 years, Ned Kelly's headless skeleton had been definitely identified. The bones were scored with bullet marks, with wounds to the left elbow (from the bullet fired by Constable Gascoigne), the lower right leg (from Sergeant Steele's shotgun blast) and the right foot. At last, the resting place of Ned Kelly had been found.

But as is often the case in the Kelly story, the solving of one mystery created another. The skull provided by Tom Baxter also underwent DNA testing. It proved that the skull was not Ned Kelly's. The whereabouts of Ned's skull are still unknown.

The discovery of the skeleton sparked a new Ned debate; where to bury him. At the time of writing, the state government and family descendants were discussing a final resting place. A Catholic service seemed likely but there was still debate on whether the remains should be buried or cremated. Many would like to see Ned's last wish granted, that he be buried by his family on consecrated ground—probably near his mother and brothers at Greta. But then there are fears his grave would become a target of vandals or even grave robbers. And others, including some in the police, worry that Ned Kelly's grave could become a shrine, a place where homage is paid to a man they see as a violent criminal. As always there are diverse views and strong feelings but there is also broad agreement that regardless of what he did, Ned Kelly should be afforded dignity and decency more than 130 years after his death.

20
THE HEALING

'Just a nice old bloke'

In Glenrowan, the ruins of Ann Jones' hotel provided a constant and unwelcome reminder of the destruction of the Kelly Gang. People went about their business as best they could but it was hard to move on from the siege when the charred evidence lay there for all to see. The gang had already become a national sensation but locally the effects were much more intimate. At the heart of the conflict were the remains of tragically wounded families, traumatised victims and a small community torn apart by a terrible event.

Although the gang had been destroyed, the grievances that had inspired the revolt remained. The families of those involved were enraged at their treatment and shamed by Ned's execution. The wider settler community burned with indignation at the treatment handed out to a man who, in their eyes, had simply demanded justice.

The newspapers reported that a new outbreak could erupt. The *Advertiser* said there were signs of another gang being formed with the aim of performing 'even more bloodthirsty outrages than were committed by the Kellys and their confederates'. *The North Eastern Ensign* revealed that Superintendent Sadleir 'quite anticipated another outbreak of the lawless inhabitants of the North-Eastern district'. He based this on the 'very great prevalence of horse stealing in the district'. There were fears that Jim Kelly or maybe Tom Lloyd would step up to lead a new Kelly Gang and that this time the bloodshed would be horrendous.

The sharing of the reward money caused more resentment; the Kelly supporters saw it as blood money and there was anger at the recipients, particularly those seen to have sinned most against the gang. There were police reports of another suit of armour being made of saw blades and the sympathisers were on the hunt for police spies. It was an uneasy time and violence could easily have broken out.

But then a policeman named Robert Graham built the first great bridge between the police and the settlers. If some of his colleagues were rogues or thugs, then Robert Graham was sensible, brave and decent. The thirty-seven-year-old had been involved in the hunt for the gang and shared in some of the reward money. When he was posted to head up a new police station at Greta in 1880, however, he fully understood that he and his three men were being asked to police a powder keg. Instead of inflaming passions, he moved to quell them. He set up a temporary headquarters on the first floor of O'Brien's Hotel—symbolically placing the police right at the heart of the unrest. Then he took time to sit down and talk with the people.

There was an uneasy calm as 1880 drew to a close, but Constable Graham continued his work as a circuit breaker when he met with Jim Kelly, the McAuliffes and other sympathiser families. He understood they were angry but managed to persuade them another outbreak would only end poorly. He did enough to ease a volatile community into the new year. Then, when Ellen Kelly came home from prison in February, Graham met with her twice—once privately and once publicly. It was an important gesture of healing. Graham had helped to prevent further violence and at the same time seemed to have understood that the unrest was more deep-seated than a simple desire for revenge. The sons and daughters of Irish, Scottish and English peasants wanted justice; specifically security of land ownership so they could build better lives in their new country.

Another policeman did much to strengthen the bridge made by Robert Graham. Henry Armstrong—one of the three police who disgraced themselves by hiding in the Sherritt hut after the shooting—was actually regarded as a brave and decent man, and he showed his true colours when he spoke to Jim Kelly soon after the siege. Jim was under close surveillance as a suspected focus for a new gang and there was a danger he might erupt. But when he and Armstrong met, Jim said he had no intention of becoming a bushranger. He had learned to be a bootmaker in prison and could make £3 a week as a respectable tradesman. He said he was 'too fond of going to theatres and taking girls into the gardens at night' to take to the bush. But Jim made it very clear what he expected in return when he told Armstrong: 'Should I ever be interfered with by the police I will not do as Ned has done; I will shoot every man and have satisfaction.'

Like his brother, Jim Kelly was not a man to accept abuse and mistreatment. Even so, Jim mostly managed to stay out of trouble. He served one more prison term, this time for stealing a horse at Cootamundra in the New South Wales Riverina, but he never took up arms against the police. He lived to old age and remained in the Greta-Glenrowan district his whole life. Older residents remember him simply as Jim Kelly, a popular and generous local man.

Bob Iskov was born in the district in 1920 and has lived there for most of his life. When he was a boy, he often saw Jim trotting past the Glenrowan schoolhouse on a grey pony. Later, during the Depression, Bob saw countless swagmen file past the same school in search of work or a handout. The swaggies walked alone or in pairs, but never in groups of three or more. The struggling farmers of the north-east tried to be generous to the men down on their luck but nobody could afford to feed three hungry mouths.

In the 'bad years', the trickle of wandering men grew. Bob Iskov remembers hearing of one swagman who called in on Jim Kelly. Jim gave the man a hunk of bread and a billy of hot water. When he saw the swagman's boots were falling to pieces, Jim offered his own shoes to the man. The swaggie protested he could not take Jim Kelly's only pair of boots but Jim insisted; he had some greenhide in the shed and he could make another pair.

In World War II, Bob Iskov enlisted in the army and fought the Japanese on the Kokoda Track in New Guinea. After doing his bit, he returned home to the north-east, where he heard that Jim wished to see him. Bob rode out to the old man's farm, where Jim presented the young ex-soldier with a black kelpie pup that Bob named Shep. Bob later got a soldier settlement farm of his own and Shep, 'the most wonderful dog', lived and worked on the farm with Bob and his young family for fourteen years, long after Jim had died.

This is how Jim Kelly is remembered by those who knew him. Not necessarily as Ned Kelly's brother, just a 'nice old bloke'.

But all that was still to come in the fragile months after the siege and there would be more pain—for both sides—before the healing could progress. This came in the form of the Kelly Royal Commission, a painful lancing of a boil that would help to bring a new beginning. There had been calls for an inquiry into the police since the outbreak began. Initially, the discontent had focused on the failure of the police to catch the gang. Then there was criticism of their decision to fire hundreds of bullets into a hotel filled with hostages. Later, there were wider questions about the operations of the police force in general. Ned Kelly had spent his years on the run trying to get the respectable public to understand why many of the poor and oppressed hated the police so much but he had only been preaching to the converted. Now even *The Argus,* which was generally supportive of the police, noted that something needed to be done.

> A reorganisation of the police force for the better control of the North-eastern district—to effect, in short, its subjugation to law and order, because that is really what has to be faced—is indeed, imperatively necessary, and this, would be greatly assisted by a searching inquiry.

In the months after the siege, the pressure for an inquiry grew to the point where it could no longer be ignored. In March 1881, the Royal Commission began hearing evidence. It sat in Benalla, Greta, Glenrowan, Beechworth, Sebastopol (Woolshed Valley) and Wangaratta. The commissioners heard evidence from sixty-four witnesses, including some of the hostages and many of the police involved in the pursuit and the siege. It was a monumental washing of dirty laundry for the police, but the commission attracted criticism for not taking any evidence from the Kellys or their supporters. A month after first sitting, however, the commission gained a powerful insight into the root cause of the unrest when it paid a remarkable visit to Ellen Kelly's home. Coverage of that visit in *The Argus* captured not only the devastation of the family but also disturbing evidence of police mistreatment.

The reporter found a 'gloomy, desolate appearance' at the Kelly home at Eleven Mile Creek. A small garden was the only

Ellen Kelly and her two grandaughters, Lil and Alice Knight, 1911.
Image courtesy of the Pictures Collection, State Library of Victoria.

land under cultivation and some of the windows were bro-ken. There was no attempt 'to make the home look homely' and there was no sign of any people present. Eventually, Ellen appeared from the back of the house and agreed to speak to the commissioners. The newspaper noted that Ellen looked care-worn but once would have been 'comely'.

She gave a damning report of the treatment of her family by the police. She said that when she was in prison and the gang was on the run, the police had dragged her children out of the house at night and used them as shields to approach other houses in search of the outlaws. The police had destroyed family possessions and spoiled their food. They had even threatened to pull down the Kelly home. Of all her persecutors, Ellen thought the Wangaratta policeman Inspector Alexander Brooke-Smith the worst behaved of the lot.

> He used to throw things out of the house and he came in once to the lock-up staggering drunk ... I wonder they allowed a man to behave as he did to an unfor-tunate woman. He wanted me to say things that were not true.

(In the Jerilderie Letter, Ned rather colourfully noted that Brooke-Smith reminded him of a 'poodle dog, half-clipped in the lion fashion'. Ned also had a poor opinion of the policeman professionally. 'He knows as much about commanding police as Captain Standish does about mustering mosquitoes and boiling them down for their fat on the backblocks of the Lachlan.')

The Argus also reported Ellen as saying the Crown would not give her title to her 35 hectares of land. If she had the title she could have the option of selling up and moving away but would prefer to stay—if the police would leave her alone. The commission then asked if any of Ellen's children wished to make a statement and the teenaged Grace was brought forward. *The Argus* noted that Grace was bashful of these fine visitors. She seemed to be about fourteen or fifteen and bore 'a much greater resemblance to her brother Ned than either Mrs Skillian or Miss Kate Kelly'. Grace was reluctant to face these important and powerful men but eventually told them that one of Ned's last requests had been for his sisters to make a statement about the family's treatment. She offered a shocking description of the persecution of defenceless women and children.

> On one occasion Detective Ward threatened to shoot me if I did not tell him where my brothers were, and he pulled out his revolver. The police used to come here and pull the things about. Mr Brooke-Smith was one of them. He used to chuck our milk, flour and honey on the floor. Once they pulled us in our nightclothes out of bed. Sergeant Steele was one of that party.

The commission eventually handed down two reports scathing of the police actions. It recommended a reorganisation of the force and penalties for many of the officers. The commissioners said Brooke-Smith was incompetent and 'should be retired'. Francis Hare gave evidence critical of his police colleagues and was censured by the commission for his troubles. The man Hare hoped to replace, Frederick Standish, was the first witness to give evidence and the commissioners found he had shown poor judgement during the outbreak. The ruthless detective Michael Ward was recommended for censure but was later promoted instead.

The commission also said Sergeant Steele should be demoted—a decision opposed by people in his home town of Wangaratta. Steele—so handy with a gun—was later presented with a sword in recognition of his work. While Steele and some of the other wrongdoers in the police were not fully held to account, Ned might have taken some satisfaction in the commission's ultimate results. Sweeping changes were enacted, creating a fair and professional police force—one Victorians could rely on. Ned had his posthumous victory.

The healing was slow and painful but one of the most important and poignant moments went largely unnoticed at the time. When Ned was lying wounded on the railway station platform, Senior Constable Kelly had asked him for the return of the gold watch that had been stolen from the dying Sergeant Kennedy at Stringybark Creek. The constable had promised to find the watch for Kennedy's widow but Ned would only reply, 'I can't tell you. I would not like to tell you.'

Wherever the watch was, it was kept safe because in 1893 a little girl—presumably a member of the Kelly family—gave the watch to William Wallace, the publican at Benalla's Broken River Hotel. Wallace, a former policeman, then returned the watch to Mrs Kennedy.

There have been three Michael Kennedys since the killings at Stringybark Creek. The oldest died in 2008. He was the father of Senior Constable Mick Kennedy, who is now stationed at Stanhope in Victoria. When the older Kennedy turned eighteen in 1937, his family presented him with the watch. Then, when Senior Constable Kennedy of Stanhope came of age thirty-three years later, the watch was handed to him. The policeman still has the watch, and amazingly, after more than 130 years, it still works. His grandson is the youngest Michael Kennedy. In 2025, when little Michael turns eighteen, he too will be given the memento of his brave ancestor.

Police came and went in Kelly Country. The Greta township faded away but Glenrowan survived, mainly thanks to its railway and its quarry. As time passed, the animosity between the police and the people faded and was gradually replaced by a mutual respect that continues today. In the 1920s, the last mounted trooper to serve at Glenrowan moved to the district. His name was John Briggs, the father of Linton Briggs who now owns the Ann Jones hotel site. Trooper John Briggs served the town faithfully and well for almost twenty-four years.

Following in the footsteps of Robert Graham, Trooper Briggs made a concerted effort to repair any lingering ill-feeling between local families and the police. He developed a bond of trust with Grace (Kelly) Griffiths and her children. It did not go unnoticed. John Briggs retired in 1955 and when he died in 1987 many locals with connections to the Kellys turned out to pay their respects. After the funeral, Ned Kelly's nephew Paddy Griffiths walked up to John Briggs' son and said: 'Linton, if they had all been like your dad we wouldn't have had all that trouble with Uncle Ned all those years ago.'

The healing was almost complete.

The descendants of the Kellys and their sympathisers soon became the respected citizens that they are today and there was no more conflict with the authorities. Ned would have been delighted to know that his sister's great-great-grandson, Anthony Griffiths, would one day become the mayor of Wangaratta. But for some, the hurt continued for generations and although the Kelly story continued to create debate and speculation across the nation, locally it was hardly discussed.

Lifelong resident Bob Iskov said some of the Kelly descendants remained bitter about the treatment of their family and their friends and neighbours did them the courtesy of minding their own business. 'It wasn't a big deal in our day,' he said. 'The Kelly story didn't really enter our heads and if the family wanted to talk about it they would, but mostly they didn't.'

Outsiders did want to talk about it, though. According to Bob Iskov this 'was a good way to get a punch in the nose' and there were cases of ill-mannered visitors getting short shrift at the pub. Journalists continued to follow the story, welcome or not, and in 1911 the reporter Brian Cookson managed to get Ellen and Jim Kelly to speak of their memories.

Cookson came to Greta and Glenrowan looking for the other side of the story 'in the defence of the outlaws'. With great foresight, Cookson noted that:

time may be when their names will be canonised in the heart of Australian boyhood. For the English people dearly love a bold and successful robber, have he anything of chivalry or courtesy about him.

Ned was undoubtedly bold, arguably successful and definitely courteous and chivalrous. Cookson was talking about the Robin Hood formula that would make Ned Kelly an Australian legend.

Cookson seemed to feel a great pity for Ellen Kelly, living in squalor and still caring for a brood of children. Here, he said, was the woman who had nursed an innocent baby who had become the greatest of outlaw figures. Her bushranger sons were dead but their mother had been 'spared to a life that is but a living death, bowed down in agonising memories, and quite devoid of hope'. Cookson saw similarities between Ellen Kelly and Ann Jones—two mothers caught up in terrible events and left with a lifetime of regret.

Kelly Country was a teeming swamp drenched by torrential rain as Cookson continued his investigation. He must have had remarkable persuasive powers because he convinced Jim Kelly to relive the family's darkest hours. In Jim, Cookson found 'a sombre-faced bushman' who nevertheless delighted in the presentation of a pony to one of his young nieces. Jim told Cookson that he had never thought of leaving the district. It was his home and there was 'the old woman' to consider. For another thing, Jim wanted to live down the infamy of his family's name.

'And it is not going wide of the mark to say that he has materially succeeded,' wrote Cookson.

No finger is pointed at him in scorn or contumely. His courage, life-long devotion, and scrupulous honesty have won him a name all to himself—and the respect of his fellow-man with it.

EPILOGUE

'Victory won by a lost battle.'

What is going to be done with the site of Ann Jones' inn? There are many ideas, ranging from doing nothing and leaving the empty block to speak for itself, to building a first-class museum where the relics of the siege and of Ann Jones' life can be displayed for all to see. Other ideas include a simple but poignant memorial—perhaps a statue or a garden. Some people would like to see a replica of the inn built in the town. Some even want it built on the site of the original, despite concerns it would devalue the significance of what happened there. It has also been suggested that the archaeology should be exposed once more and covered with armoured glass so visitors can walk over the ruins of the inn to gain a greater understanding of the bush pub where history was made. At the time of writing, a decision had not been made.

The grass has now grown back on the narrow block, the Glenrowan Inn sign has been re-erected and the pony has returned. The fig tree still grows there, the statues of Steve and

Dan stand guard at the front fence and the uniformed police are attacking. The visitors still cross the rail bridge to stand against the fence and ponder what went on here. Some can imagine gunfire and screams echoing through the years and others can only shrug and ask: Is this all there is?

After they have looked at the site, the visitors might cross the bridge back to the main street, where they could grab a snack or a Kelly souvenir. Some will then take the northern exit out of town, past the new police station and on to the Hume Freeway towards the New South Wales border. Within an hour or so Kelly Country is just a fading glimpse in the rear view mirror. The others will head south, under the watchful gaze of Big Ned and on to the highway towards Melbourne, where Ned Kelly's turbulent life came to an end.

He had lived for less than twenty-six years, yet in that short time his actions cemented his place in the foundations of a nation's identity. Ironically, it was at around the time of Ned's birth that a group of miners created another foundation myth when they took up arms at the Eureka Stockade. The visiting American author Mark Twain would later describe the gunfight at Eureka as 'another instance of a victory won by a lost battle'. It took a few generations,but eventually the same could be said of Ned Kelly's Last Stand at Glenrowan. It's one of the reasons that so many people now travel to see the place where the Last Stand occurred.

Some will leave Glenrowan with a new opinion of Ned but most will have already made up their minds. We will continue to argue whether he was hero or villain, but the truth is he was both. Ned Kelly is what we make him. To some, he was a hero in 1880 and is a hero now—an even greater one immortalised by death and his own glorious actions. Others can only see him as a villain—a thief, an armed robber and a killer when he lived—and a villain today. But he is a defining figure for all Australians and somehow his failure at Glenrowan was ultimately a success. Partly thanks to Ned and what he did at the Glenrowan Inn more than 130 years ago, Australians became 'as game as Ned Kelly' and we still hold dear the concept of a fair go.

SELECTED REFERENCES

Books

Australian Son, Max Brown, 1948, Georgian House, Melbourne

The Briars and Thorns, Joseph Ashmead, 1923, unpublished

Bushrangers: Australia's Greatest Self-made Heroes, Evan McHugh, 2011, Penguin, Melbourne

Catching the Kellys, Thomas Carrington (edited by Ian Jones), 2003, Lothian Pty Ltd, Melbourne

The Complete Inner History of the Kelly Gang and their Pursuers, J J Kenneally, 1929, Reviewers Pty Ltd, Melbourne

I am Ned Kelly, John Moloney, 1980, Melbourne University Press, Melbourne

I Was at the Kelly Gang Roundup, Judith Douthie, 2008, Network Creative Services, Greensborough, Victoria

The Last of the Bushrangers, Francis Hare, 1892, Hurst & Blackett, London

Ned and the Others, Dagmar Balcarek and Gary Dean, 1995, Glen Rowen Cobb & Co, Glenrowan

Ned Kelly: A Short Life, Ian Jones, 1995, Lothian Pty Ltd, Melbourne

The Ned Kelly Encyclopedia, Justin Corfield, 2003, Thomas C Lothian, South Melbourne

Ned Kelly's Last Days, Alex C Castles and Jennifer Castles, 2005, Allen & Unwin, Sydney

Recollections of a Victorian Police Officer, John Sadleir, 1913, George Robertson and Company, Melbourne

Archives/images

State Library of Victoria

Television documentaries

Besieged, The Ned Kelly Story, Film Projects, 2003. Directors Gregory Miller and Barrie Dowdall.

Ned Kelly Uncovered, Renegade Films, 2009. Director Alex West.

Outlawed, The Real Ned Kelly, Windfall Films, 2003. Director Mark Lewis.

Newspapers/journals

The Age

The Argus

Australasian Sketcher

The Border Mail

The Daily Telegraph

Herald Sun

Meanjin
The North Eastern Ensign
The Ovens and Murray Advertiser
Cookson Series (*The Sun*)
The Sydney Morning Herald

Internet
bailup.com
glenrowan1880.com
ironoutlaw.com
kellygang.asn.au
nedkellysworld.com.au

ACKNOWLEDGEMENTS

The writing of a book is rarely the work of one person alone. There isn't room to thank everyone who helped to make this book a reality, but special mention must be made of those whose enthusiasm and dedication enabled it to move from daydream to fact. It's often said that a book could not have been written without the help of so-and-so. In my case, this book definitely would not have happened without the help of Ian Jones, who shared his passion for the Kelly story and patiently added suggestions, corrections and wise counsel. Thank you, Ian—truly a scholar and a gentleman.

Thanks also to Adam Ford and his team—not only for their professionalism and warm welcome to their project—but also for all the laughs along the way. Who would have thought that digging holes in the ground could be such fun?

My friends and colleagues, Reece Rayner and Neal Kelly, did more than they know to help. Cheers, boys.

To the owner of the siege site, Linton Briggs, thank you for sharing your remarkable little corner block with the rest of Australia.

The support and co-operation of Heritage Victoria, the State Library of Victoria and the Rural City of Wangaratta was invaluable. So too was the input of Tim Murray, Professor of Archaeology at La Trobe University.

In a broader sense, my gratitude goes out to the Kelly fans and foes (especially the descendants of those who were there) for sharing the stories of their ancestors so willingly. And the people of Glenrowan and the rest of the north-east deserve special acknowledgement for sharing their stories and their beautiful part of the world. Thanks to all.

But most of all, thank you to Kim and Jimmy for their love and support.

ABOUT THE AUTHOR

Paul Terry is a producer with 7 Prime, and has worked as a journalist in radio, television and newspapers in New South Wales, South Australia and Tasmania. He was part of the archaeological survey of the Kelly Gang siege site in Glenrowan, and subsequently worked as a producer on the documentary *Ned Kelly Uncovered*, which aired on ABC TV.